THE BLACK MAN'S GUIDE OUT OF POVERTY

For Black Men Who Demand Better

By

Aaron Clarey

To Ken and Mike

"Security is security"

Table of Contents

Part I

Part II

PART I
AN UNACCEPTABLE SITUATION

INTRODUCTION

A Welcomed Development

A funny thing was happening.

My blog, You Tube, podcast, Facebook, Twitter and all other manners of social media accounts were experiencing a booming increase in readership and followership from an unlikely group of people. Up until this point my extremely right-leaning, libertarian-themed blog attracted the usual suspects:

White male Republicans
NRA types
Nerdy economists
College kids who thought libertarianism was "cool"
Aspiring players
Silver bugs
The occasional Asian engineer,
and
Traditional women who didn't mind being housewives.

But something had happened and I was now attracting what was no doubt my fastest growing demographic – black males.

At first I thought maybe it was just a brief phenomenon. Perhaps a young conservative black man was merely sharing me with his other conservative black friends. Maybe the libertarian college group in a predominantly black college discovered my works. But upon further investigation, I realized it was something much more fundamental. Much more permanent. Much more universal. And much more real:

Black men had had enough.

And not only did they have enough, they were now searching for alternative explanations as to their positions and lives in America. And be it through word of mouth, internet searches, or what have you, they were landing on my blog, podcast, and You Tube channel.

This was a welcomed development for several reasons. One, I

always love increased readership and viewership as it just means more money for me. Two, I was happy to see a group that is normally associated with leftist politics entertain and listen to libertarian/conservative ideas. Three, my views about the free market, self-reliance, excellence over affirmative action, stable families, etc., were not immediately dismissed as "racist" or "bigoted," but rather entertained. And, four (the real reason this was such a welcomed development) is that it showed black men were no longer believing the lies told to them by the powers that be and were now open to alternative ideas about finances, prosperity, happiness, love and life.

Alternative ideas that would once and for all truly set them free.

It is my sincere and true belief that black men are on the precipice of the greatest potential advancement in their entire history of the black race since emancipation. However, instead of breaking the physical shackles that binded them to slavery, they are about to break the mental ones that have condemned them to an effective second class citizenship. And when these shackles are broken, black men (and any other man for that matter) can become truly unlimited in their potential. They will not only be able to close the various economic gaps between whites, but surpass them, even surpassing Asian standards of living if they so choose. They will be able to eliminate crime, poverty, and various other sociological ailments currently plaguing black males. They will also be able to build strong families, live enjoyable lives, and longer lives on top of it. In short, it is now within the power and ability of every black man to improve their lives in nearly every aspect as they are about to accurately identify and diagnose the problems that are holding them back.

But do not think it will be easy.

In order to truly benefit from this book you will need to rethink everything you've thought. Question everything you've been told. And above all else commit yourself to empiricism, unbiased thinking, and a desire to discover and know the truth. Not only will this challenge your previously established world-view (and thus threaten the mental comfort, security, and pride that comes with it), but you can fully expect to alienate some of your peers, begetting accusations of being an "Uncle Tom" or an "Oreo" or a traitor to the cause.

You can also fully expect every imaginable accusation of racism, bigotry, misogyny, etc., will be hurled my way. This book threatens not just the pride and egos of many people, but threatens people in power who rely on keeping blacks down for their own political gain. And this book directly threatens their power.

I only ask three things of you:

1. Entertain these ideas. You do not have to believe them, but I merely ask you give them a chance IN THEIR ENTIRETY and judge them for yourself afterwards. If you do not like them, fine. You can simply discard them and burn the book if you desire. But at least hear them out before breaking out the gasoline and matches.

2. Understand I am not racist. An asshole? Sure, but not a racist. I view all men as equals and judge them by their achievements and accomplishments. Not the pigmentation in the skin.

3. Believe me when I say that my intention is to help black men. I have no ulterior motive other than to capitalize and realize what I think is possible. Yes, I will probably make a little money on book sales, but I would love nothing more than to see the black community have standards of living on par with whites, not to mention expose the people who have been truly oppressing the black community for nearly six decades.

If we operate from these premises of trust, more can be achieved in the hours it will take to read this book than the decades of failed political promises.

How to Use This Book

The issue of black poverty is not simply one of dispensing the same old standard financial advice that you can find in any library book. The black community and black males in particular have a unique situation that further complicates the issue. Because of this "The Black Man's Guide Out of Poverty" is broken down into two parts.

Part 1 addresses the psychological, philosophical, political and economic hurdles to success black men face, while Part 2 provides the literal financial instructions and steps you can take to escape poverty. However, this second part is not your run of the mill "financial advice" that tells you to go to college, invest in an IRA, get life insurance, etc. It is tailored for black men who are in the lower income classes with recommendations and advice specific to that situation.

However, you have an option when it comes to Part 2 of the book. I have written a much more thorough and complete financial advice book that is specifically for men ("Bachelor Pad Economics"). It covers nearly 97% of the material in this book, minus the racial theme and intention of helping out black males specifically. Depending on your interest and inclination you may want to consider purchasing that book and using it as a substitute for Part 2 of this one. However, Part 2 is thorough and complete enough to stand on its own, and suffices for the purposes of this book. If you are interested, however, you can find "Bachelor Pad Economics" on Amazon.com.

Regardless of which route you choose, it is important to read Part 1 of this book first. It lays down the theory and philosophical foundation and arguments for the second part, and as it just so happens is the most important part of this book. The reason is that while anybody can follow literal instructions, unless they understand the underlying strategy or philosophy for those instructions, they never really learn to do it on their own. Additionally, understanding the overarching purpose of a strategy or philosophy allows you to teach yourself or trouble shoot problems on your own, without having to rely on an instruction manual. To that end, I recommend reading the first part thoroughly and using the second part (or Bachelor Pad Economics) as more of a reference book to be consulted on issues specific to your situation.

CHAPTER 1
THE BLACK MAN'S PLIGHT

Statistics

The plight of black males and the black community at large is not one of opinion, myth, politics, hyperbole or rhetoric. It is real. By nearly every measure of standards of living, health, wealth, etc., blacks rank at the bottom or tie for the bottom (typically with native Americans).

In terms of economics blacks suffer incomes of roughly only 2/3rds that of their white counterparts. Because of this lower income, they have less money saved up for retirement, not to mention much lower home-ownership rates. Complicating matters is an unemployment rate that has historically ran at double that of whites.

Economics	White	Black
Income per capita	$30,723	$19,227
Median wage	$55,412	$32,229
Median wealth	$110,973	$10,824
Avg. retirement savings	$115,991	$5,568
Unemployment rate	5.1%	11%
Home Ownership	72.6%	42.9%

In education black males do not fare any better. While whites can expect over 3/4ths of their male population to graduate from high school, nearly 50% of black males drop out of high school. This is in part reflected in lower standardized test scores (such as the SAT) which only compromises a young man's college prospects and thus, future earnings potential. Worse still, black men do not earn a proportional percentage of STEM (Science, Technology, Engineering and Math) degrees. While they account for a full 12% of the population, they only earn 6% of the degrees in these vital fields.

Education	White	Black
SAT scores	527	428
High school graduate %	78%	52%
% w/ bachelors degree	30.9%	17.7%

%STEM Degree/% pop.   66.9%/74%   6.1%/12%

The family life of black men is sadly chaotic, even non-existent. While divorce rates between blacks and whites are more or less on par with one another, a large part of this is due to the lack of marriage in the black community in the first place. However, this has not prevented blacks from pro-creating resulting in 72% of their children being born out of wedlock. This added stress of single-parenthood does not bode well for members of this now dysfunctional family structure. Black children suffer thrice the rates of abuse, while adults suffer twice the domestic violence in both male-to-female and female-to-male oriented violence. Sadly, young black boys are often brought up in this hostile environment, resulting in an uphill battle throughout life, fraught with higher rates of suicide, crime, depression, alcoholism and many other societal ills.

Sociological/Family	White	Black
Divorce Rate	10	12
Illegitimate birth	29.1%	72.3%
Child abuse (state of CA)	7.7/1000	24/1000
DV male-to-female	8%	20%
DV female-to-male	10%	22%

These stressors and disadvantages no doubt take a toll on black men's health. Life expectancy for black men is the lowest of nearly all racial and sexual categories, a full four years less than their white male counterparts. Additionally, it is not just the length of life, but quality of life that suffers as well. Black males report being in "fair" or "poor" health at a rate nearly twice that of whites. Making matters worse STD's are most prevalent in the black community where blacks suffer the highest infection rates of all racial groups.

Health	White	Black
Life expectancy (men)	74	70
Percent of HIV Positive	34.6	46.1
Gonorrhea	30x's higher rate in blacks than whites	
% "In fair or poor health"	8.9%	15%

Finally, it is not just the health of black men that suffers from this disadvantaged youth. With more domestic violence, more child abuse, the absence of fathers, and the consequential lack of discipline that comes with it, black men are simply more prone to crime. Though black men only make up 12% of the population they account for 40% of the prison population. They suffer incarceration rates eight times that of whites, and one in every two black men will be arrested before turning 23.

Crime	White	Black
Homicide rate		8x's whites
Arrested before 23	38%	50%
Incarceration rate		8x's whites

We could go on and certainly entire books could be written about what causes these problems, but the point is that black males as a whole have harder lives than nearly every other racial and sexual group. It's not a theory. It's not a lie. It's not propaganda. It's not whining. It's not playing the victim. Black males are the most suffered group in the United States today.

The "Total" Costs

The problem with looking at these statistics is they are mere fleeting glances at specific points in time into the status and experiences of black men. They do not look back in time to calculate and consider what the cumulative social, time, economic, and financial costs have been. And while citing statistics might make people aware there's a problem, it isn't until you take the time to calculate the total costs sustained over history do you develop an urgency or sympathy for black men and the black community.

The costs are simply staggering.

The most notable cost is the amount of years lost due to lower life expectancies. Since 1865 black men have cumulatively lost 169.2 million years against white males. This translates to an effective equivalent of 2.6 million *total* lives lost. Though certainly not the majority of the total male black population that has lived in the US, it makes one wonder just what could have been achieved with these theoretical 2.6 million additional lives.

With shorter life expectancies, combined with historic racism, educational attainment, etc., black men have not been able to make as much as whites, historically earning only 63 cents on the dollar. When this is amortized over the history of the emancipated black man, there is a shortage of $16.2 TRILLION in cumulative earnings (in today's dollars). Naturally with lower earnings there is less opportunity to save and invest. This has further cost black men over $2.8 TRILLION in historical savings.

It is no surprise with lower income and wealth black males have suffered the commensurate poverty that comes with it. And poverty is one of the key determinants of crime. Today black men account for 40% of the US prison population and have accounted for a disproportionate percentage in the past. The tragedy is even though they are still alive and able-bodied men, they are sitting stagnant in a jail cell, unable to capitalize on life and it's opportunities. And while the data is not terribly precise I estimate that black men have cumulative served nearly 6 million years in prison. This is equal to 91,500 life equivalents, nearly the population of Green Bay.

Finally, as is often the consequence of incarceration - fatherless families. Between poverty, crime, and a whole host of other sociological and economic reasons, black children suffer the scourge of single-parent households and absentee fathers. 28 million black children, nearly half the entire historical American population of blacks have been born out of wedlock.

It isn't until you look at these total costs do you understand the enormity and severity of the problems facing black men today.

(*It should be noted these costs are merely estimates as there are some obvious mathematical difficulties in calculating these figures for a population that has changed and grown since 1865. Some of these difficulties include estimating the total number of blacks that have lived in the US **throughout time,** inflation, changing incarceration rates, the slowly closing gaps in life expectancies and income, etc. The above figures are a "best effort" attempt and any further refinement of the figures would be appreciated*).

Victims in Another, Unspoken, Horrific Regard

But whether you look at current statistics or cumulative historical ones, it still does not speak to what is arguably the worst atrocity facing black men today. Worse than the 6.5% shorter life expectancy. Worse than the $16.2 trillion in lost income. Worse than 70% being born into with world outside of wedlock. It is the complete theft and, consequently, destruction of their one and finite lives.

At first this may seem a bit hyperbolic, merely an exaggeration to overstate a case. Yet make no mistake about it, their lives are being destroyed in one very key and unspoken regard. But in order to understand how we first must understand what life is all about. And in order to do that a person needs to understand what I like to call "The Ultimate Context."

Understand most people born into this world live it in a boring, monotonous haze. They do what most other people do. They think what most other people think. And very rarely do they ever take the time to sit down, truly think things through and ask what is the best use of this one and finite life that has been given to them. Complicating matters, as people age they take on more and more responsibilities such as a job, children, a mortgage and other obligations to the point they simply don't have time to ponder and answer these important life questions. Thus, by the time they have the time and freedom to think about these things, it's already too late. The majority of their lives have been led, the majority of opportunities wasted, nothing can be done to bring back the past, and their own mortality is staring them in the face, rapidly approaching. The consequence, sadly, is that the vast majority of people die not knowing why they were living in the first place. And thus their lives are like all others – common, unexceptional, mundane, and ultimately wasted.

Thankfully, the secret to life, the secret to happiness can be explained by taking the time to think things through and put life in its "ultimate context." Ask why you are here, what is the point and purpose of life, and, most importantly, what makes you happy in life? And what you will inevitably find out is that

the point and purpose of life,
the reason you are here,
the true one and only sole source of happiness is...

other people.

Many men scoff at this idea, thinking it's money or power. Many women laugh at this idea thinking it's glamor or fame. But in the end if you think about it enough you will come to the undeniable conclusion that the only thing that matters in life is...

other people.

The perfect example I always use is video games.

Say you have the latest, most advanced video game console, replete with all the games you could ever want and the most pimped out sound system to boot. No matter how advanced and complex that system is, it is still a finite, limited entity. Yes you can play the video games. Yes the graphics are grand. But in the end that video gaming system is not conscious, it is not sentient. It is merely an elaborate construct of wires and plastic programmed to behave in a set, limited, and finite way.

Humans on the other hand are infinite. Not so much in life expectancy, but in terms of their potential interactions and reactions. A human is dynamic, changing one minute to the next. It is conscious, it's sentient, and it has its own mind which means it's infinitely more interesting, engaging and challenging than a mere "PS4" or X Box One." Additionally, they are truly interactive. They are just as self-aware as you and, thusly, are able to challenge, converse with, and provoke thought in you. But above all else, they are able to prompt emotions such as love, anger, embarrassment, humor and laughter in others. Because of this they are the only thing you can truly bond with and care for, making them the most important thing in the world. Alas, this is why playing video games on your own is certainly fun, but playing it with friends either online or at home is a blast.

But out of the now seven billion humans that populate the planet only a select handful of them are going to be the ones that you let into your life. Your family, your friends, your loved ones, etc. Consequently, these key people will provide you with nearly all of your happiness, fun, love, joy and purpose in life. However, even within this tight knit group of people there is really only going to be one person who you will derive the majority of your happiness and joy from, and that person is your wife.

Whether you like it or not, and whether you have intentions to marry or not, your wife WILL BE the single largest source of happiness (and sometimes pain) in your life. And the reason you have no choice in the matter has nothing to do with romanticism, love, or sexual attraction. It's psychology.

Understand through millions of years of evolution you are biologically, genetically, and physically hardwired to derive the most amount of happiness and joy from a woman you love. You are mentally pre-programmed to be happiest with a wife. Yes, you may not have a woman you're enamored with now. Yes, you may have no intentions of ever marrying. And you could be perfectly content and happy with your swinging, player, bachelor life just as it is right now. But should you theoretically run into a woman that is so beautiful, kind, compatible, engaging, and loving that you're compelled to propose, there is no point in your life you'll be happier than when you are with that woman.

Naturally, the consequence of finding such a rare woman has historically been children. And these children, just like your wife, will also become the largest source of happiness (and sometimes pain) in your life. This then constitutes your very own "family" which has not only served as the basic building block of all societies since time immemorial, but the primary source of your love, care, joy, happiness, and purpose in life.

There's just one minor problem.

Right now you likely find the concept or the idea of having a loving, reliable wife laughable. Add wonderful, adoring children and you're probably spitting milk through your nose. I might as well throw in a nice house in the suburbs, a six figure salary, an SUV, a sports car and a case of gold bullion while we're at it. And the reason it's laughable is because all men of all colors face the same problem in the United States:

The quality of women is just absolute shit.

This is not an opinion. This is not sexism. This is not "misogyny."

It's just the plain damn truth.

Women today are spoiled, they are manipulative, they are entitled, they are arrogant, they are lazy and many of them are mentally unstable. Consequently, the vast majority of them are woefully inadequate when it comes to marriage material. And while women may take umbrage or offense to that, it does not change the fact that this is empirically so. Men today are proposing less, and if they do, they usually postpone marriage until they're well into their 30's. Men are also doing away with marriage altogether, preferring instead to cohabitate or just date. And your laughing at the prospect of a "loving, reliable wife" is visceral proof of the low quality of women because it's a borderline fairy tale. No matter how disagreeable women may find the above accusation, the truth is men no longer view them as viable candidates for marriage or motherhood.

But pause for a moment and think about how sad and pathetic that really is.

Permit yourself once to imagine you could find a wife who was kind, loving, caring and attractive. Imagine a couple of kids who are well-behaved and want nothing more than to jump into daddy's arms when he comes home. Imagine a nice warm fire and dinner with the family on Christmas Eve night. And imagine sending your kids to grandma's while you and the Mrs. go to Vegas and you take advantage of her beautiful physique which she kept in shape just for you. The real tragedy is not that you live five years less than white men. It's not that you and your ancestors' lost share of income would likely purchase you a house today. It's that this "fairy tale life" we mock and ridicule was once the standard, but is no longer possible today. It's that your one, primary source of happiness - your family -

has been stolen from you and so corrupted that the concept is one we depressingly laugh at.

The question is who destroyed the most important thing in your life? Who stole your family? Who took your women and turned them from Lena Horne into Whoopi Goldberg? Who took this one thing that would give your life meaning, purpose and happiness, regardless of the disadvantages you may have been born into?

The answer may shock you because it is the people who've been claiming to help you this entire time.

It's the state, aka "the government."

Your Real Enemy

At first this may sound conspiratorial, if not just outright wrong.

"The government that has instituted affirmative action? The government that got us the Civil Rights Act? The state that pays for housing, food, education and health care? This government is to blame for all our problems when it's been helping us this entire time? That's our enemy? That's our oppressor?"

Counter-intuitive as that may sound, it's true. And the reason is in the "Law of Unintended Consequences."

No matter how well-intended, no matter how noble a law or a piece of legislation is meant to be, many times the good intentions of honest, well-meaning statesmen are not enough to improve the lives of the people they're trying to help. Sadly, more often than not these well-intended policies often prove damaging to the intended beneficiaries because either something was overlooked or somebody failed to anticipate the full consequences of these actions. And thus was the case in "The Great Society" from the 1960's.

The Great Society was, in its simplest form, an attempt to eliminate poverty and discrepancies in standards of living between various races, sexes, and other groups of people. The intention was very noble and the solution was very simple – give these disadvantaged groups money and other advantages so they can get a leg up and overtime be on par with the rest of society. But while seemingly simple and patently noble, it was a highly flawed strategy because it was too easy to be taken advantage of. And as the Law of Unintended Consequences predicted, it was.

Politicians quickly realized that by promising people money they could simply bribe people to vote for them. Also, unscrupulous people realized if they were considered "disadvantaged" they could be on the receiving end of this money. At first it was people consciously scamming the system, and politicians willingly paying them for the added votes. But over the course of three decades and three generations a culture and mentality was engrained where people were now living off this system with no shame or even awareness of what they were doing. Matter of fact, so engrained had this mentality become, most people were unconscious of the parasitic nature of their lifestyle. Money just "came from the government" and that's how you lived your life.

Naturally, there was resistance from taxpayers footing the bill for this. So in order to keep selling this "money for votes" racket to the voting public politicians cleverly tugged at their heart strings by highlighting two desperate groups of people that were in dire need of government support – women and children. Specifically, single mothers and their children.

And it is here where the government stole our birthright and destroyed our families.

Previous to The Great Society, the basic unit of society was the family, and the nucleus of the family was the man. The man was the breadwinner, he was the head of the household, and he was the final arbiter of all major decisions. However, with all of these rights came great responsibilities. He had to make sure his family didn't starve. He had to work extra hours if money was short. He had to fix the car. He had to repair the house, keeping it in good order, ensuring his family was safe from weather, thieves and all other external threats. He had to discipline the children, train them and instruct them. And if necessary he was to die for them should any member of his family be threatened. In exchange for this he was given not only the love, but the loyalty and *support* of his wife, as well as the right to raise his children as he saw fit.

But now, for the first time in US history, the government was supplanting his role. A woman no longer needed a man. Not because she had a job or was pursuing a career, but because the government would cut her a check. And not only would the state cut her a check, but it would cut her more checks the more kids she had. Soon it wasn't the husband paying for health insurance, rent, food, education and gas, but the state through it's ever increasing numbers of social programs, all designed to help those "poor single mothers and their children."

The ultimate consequence of these "well-intended" programs was that it destroyed the basic unit of society – the family – by removing the man and replacing him with a government check. Sadly, this removal of men from society resulted in the aforementioned "unintended consequences" which have done nothing short of wreak unimaginable destruction and devastation upon US families, especially those in the black community.

The biggest casualties are arguably children. No longer required to stay together for the betterment of their children, women can now simply "divorce" their husbands on grounds as flimsy as "I'm not happy." And it is not so much that divorce law changed allowing women to divorce more easily, as much as it is the knowledge that the government will financially provide for her and her children, making the man doubly unnecessary. Even worse, the fact 70% of black children are born out of wedlock suggests black women do not even view the man as a potential father, husband or head-of-household type figure. They simply view him as a "sperm donor," leaving said roles to the government. Regardless of being a single mom on purpose or through divorce, the children are not raised in a stable, reliable nuclear family.

Another way children suffer is due to the lack of the father's presence in the household. Here a whole host of problems arise without the presence of a dad to raise his children. Since there is no "ultimate authority" capable of physically forcing discipline, behavior, and respect upon children, they grow up ill-reared, disrespectful, borderline feral, increasing chances of crime and lowering chances of a good career. Children are also reared in a skewed manner as 100% of the rearing is done by the mother or their predominantly female elementary school teachers. This not only leaves them ill-prepared when it comes time to dealing with the male half of society, but results in weak, pansified, whiny kids who are emotional, thin-skinned and incapable of criticism or challenge (just look at today's modern hipsters or "Social Justice Warriors"). Finally, children just simply suffer emotionally and psychologically without having their dad around no matter what various "authorities" or "experts" say.

Cutting men out of the family also affected the finances of not just the family unit, but the country. Previous to the "replacement," men were at least a control valve when it came to women's spending. There was a family budget, there was limited income, and you could not just "buy anything you wanted." The family had to live within their means, teaching everybody fiscal discipline. However, with this control valve gone and a metaphorical "blank government check" available, women are now allowed to spend money however they please. This has resulted not only in instances where single moms buy designer clothes (but not food for their babies), but an enormous increase in taxation (which men disproportionately pay). Alas, men are still effectively footing the bill, but with no control or say on how said monies are spent.

Akin to frivolous spending, government replacing men has allowed women to become more promiscuous. Obviously, a real husband would adamantly refuse his wife to have sex with other men. But a government check is perfectly accepting of an open relationship. This allows women the option of having their cake and eating it too. Not only can they have children without the "annoyance" of being married and answering to a husband, but a government-husband substitute will allow her to sleep with as many men as she wants. This does not so much mean women will nail every hot bad boy, thug that comes along (though they will) as much as it makes "settling down and marrying" a less attractive option (as well as makes divorce a more attractive one).

Worse than promiscuity, however, is just how much government programs have spoiled women, making them completely un-marriagable. If you were raised with a father you were likely held to standards and expectations. Additionally, you were likely taught to consider others, respect others and how to get along with others (especially men). And the reason your father taught you these things was not so that you would become altruistic, but so you could function in the real world. Purely selfish people cannot function in the real world. You need to consider others and adhere to a certain level of ethics, standards and expectations. But a government check has no such standards. A government check has no such expectations. A government check is merely a non-sentient piece of paper incapable of rearing, disciplining or imparting wisdom.

Unfortunately, girls brought up by a government check and not a father lack the ability to sympathize, be selfless, consider others, etc. (boys as well, but we are obviously interested in women). They can also be quite demanding claiming "my man better do this, and make that, and bring home this," despite them never achieving anything of their own or having a right to demand such things. Ultimately, these traits are incompatible with marriage as the only way marriage works is if you love the other person more than yourself. Sadly, as more and more people are reared without fathers, this selflessness declines and the pool of marriagable candidates (and thus our chance for genuine happiness) shrinks.

Finally, (and perhaps the most ironic cost replacing men with government has had on women) is one of unrealistic expectations. If you take the average man and what he can offer a woman, and compare it to the government and what it can offer a woman, there just isn't any comparison. No man of any race can compete. The average man with his $45,000 a year job, 10 year old GM car and average looks cannot compete against the trillions of dollars President Obama, your state governor, and local county commissioner are willing to offer women. They're willing to pay for a girl's food, her health care, her education, her housing, her children, her transportation, everything (all one has to do is look at the political campaign "Julia" to see just how much the government is willing to provide for women http://l.barackobama.com/truth-team/entry/the-life-of-julia/). Worse still, the government will hold her to absolutely no standards while you will. You'll (rightly) insist she remain loyal, stay in shape, carry her weight, treat you kindly, help raise the children, etc., while politicians just want one thing and one thing only – her vote.

There are certainly other costs society has suffered due to men being replaced by the government, but the larger point is clear. Men, particularly black men, have had the most important thing in their lives taken from them by the state. With no wife and no family to look forward to, a man has little purpose in life. This has relegated them to pursue an alternative life different than what their forefathers did and what they're genetically programmed to do. Of course, this alternative life certainly has its benefits - perpetual bachelorhood, minimal expenses, video games, friends, meaningless flings, easy job, etc., - but sadly, it is ultimately a pointless one, resulting in a listless life void of true agency and purpose. And when you add to this all the other ailments and disadvantages black men endure it is a problem that must be recognized, must be admitted, and above all else, diagnosed correctly so that it may be solved. Too many lives depend on it.

You Deserve a Better Life

The most important lesson I try to convey to my clients or students is "finiteness." The reason is that it puts life in its "Ultimate Context." And it does this by getting people to understand that their life, their consciousness, their self-awareness, and sentienceness will end. You will go from having this conscious thought reading this book and seeing the world around you one second, and the next second it will be black. It will be over. You will die. It will go dark and you won't return to where you came from pre-birth, because there was no you pre-birth. You will simply cease to exist and all your experiences will be lost forever to the fates of time.

For whatever reason, you were born and put on this planet. And no matter what disadvantages you may have been born into, this one and finite life of yours is yours alone. You have an estimated 71 incredibly short years in a universe that has been around for five billion. You can do what you please with it.

The ultimate question every man, black or not, must ask himself is what do you want to do with it?

Do you want to do what everybody else has done, achieving nothing of note or uniqueness?
Do you want to do what you are told, serving the lives of others and not yours?
Do you want to continue living your life as you have been knowing nothing will change?
Are you going to accept this is as good as it gets, resigning the rest of your life to one of poverty, mediocrity, and what society has "determined" you will have?

Or will you demand better from this one, finite, precious, and incredibly short life you have?

Naturally, since you're reading this book, you're demanding a better life. You're sick of your current lot in life, you're not going to lead the same life everybody else is, and you're going to do what you can to make it better. However, it's not simply a matter of "wishing" for one or "demanding" one. It's going to take work, it's going to take effort, and it's going to take quite a lot of thinking and philosophizing. But before you can even embark on that path, before you can take that first step towards a better life, you need to do something that is absolutely necessary and vital:

You need to accurately diagnose the problem.

If you fail to do this, it's very simple. Your problems won't be solved. And no matter how hard you work at it, 100% of your efforts will all be wasted. Ergo, the first question we have to ask is a simple, but critical one:

Is what the black community doing working?
Is what *YOU'RE* doing working?

In the introduction to this book, I wrote:

"In order to truly benefit from this book you will need to rethink everything you've thought. Question everything you've been told. And above all else commit yourself to empiricism, unbiased thinking,

and a desire to discover and know the truth."

And it is here we need to commit ourselves to honestly assessing the problem. Because if you want your feelings not to be hurt, Oprah is right over there. If you want success, you need to face, accept and live in reality. Your life is just too short and too precious otherwise.

CHAPTER 2
THE TRUTH SHALL SET YOU FREE

The Reality Principle

Before we embark on this chapter it is important to understand The Reality Principle. Not only will it help you in your endeavors to escape poverty, but will help in nearly every other aspect of your life.

The Reality Principle is very simple. It is the FACT that if you base your decisions in reality, they will be more effective and successful. The further away from reality you base your decisions, the less effective and successful you will be. For example, say I want to climb a 15,000 ft mountain. The reality is that it is quite the physical challenge, not only requiring that I be in peak physical shape, but also adapt to the altitude so I do not get altitude sickness. If I decide to train first, doing smaller mountains, increasing my cardio, as well as spend some time in a higher altitude town to adapt to the lack of oxygen, chances are I will be successful in climbing the mountain. However, if I am impatient and think that I can just run up the mountain with no training I will fail miserably, either being physically incapable of climbing the mountain or succumbing to the altitude sickness that is sure to ensue.

At first The Reality Principle may not seem to be anything special. It's little more than common sense. But the real value of The Reality Principle is not it's simple logic, but whether you adhere to it and (this is key)

commit to it in spite of your psychological and emotional preferences.

The perfect example, if not the epitome of The Reality Principle, is fat women.

The reality is that men are not physically attracted to fat women. "Logic" would then suggest that women would accept this as fact and, in order to attract men, lose weight and go to the gym. However, that would require women:

1. Admit they're fat,
2. Go to the gym
and
3. Diet

While a small percentage of women do this, the majority do something quite different – they rationalize and lie to themselves.

Instead of basing their decisions in the reality that men do not find fat women attractive and that to be thin you have to go to the gym, their brains conduct insane levels of mental acrobatics, lying to themselves to avoid these facts.

"Well, I'll just eat four cookies instead of five."
"Well, I'll go for a 10 minute 'power walk.'"
"Well, I'll lift these small puny weights for 10 minutes."

Worse still, some are so delusional they will try to completely redefine reality, claiming men should be ashamed for liking hot chicks and that fat is sexy.

"Big is beautiful!"
"Men should like you for you!"
"I'm 'body positive'!" (look it up)
"You must accept Fat Acceptance!" (look it up)
"I don't care what men think!"

But regardless of what lies and rationalizations they tell themselves, in the end they still fail. They're still fat, they're still unattractive, and no guy is going to want to date them. And it's all because they did not have the courage to base their decisions in reality and the willpower to follow through on those decisions.

But before we go slamming on fat women, we have to admit that EVERYBODY to some degree or another fails to adhere to The Reality Principle.

For example, the key to success with women is working out and asking thousands of them out, the majority of which are going to shoot you down. The Reality Principle would dictate you spend hours at the gym and learn not to let it affect you personally when a woman rejects you. But men will exercise equally erroneous mental acrobatics in the hopes there's an alternative way to avoid that pain. Some will dress nice, hoping women do the approaching. Some will try sitting next to a girl in class, but never pull the trigger and ask her out. Others will approach women, but never see the inside of a gym. And some will just preemptively write women off completely, protecting their ego by saying, "American women suck" or "all they want is money."

Regardless of whether you're a man or a woman, adhering to The Reality Principle may suck, it may be painful, and it may hurt your pride. But it is the most direct route to success because ONLY decisions based in reality lead to success. And the same applies whether it's climbing mountains, losing weight, or getting out of poverty. You need to accept reality, base you decisions in that reality, and follow through with them regardless of your predispositions. Otherwise, all of this is theoretical and ineffective.

Two Competing Theories

Using The Reality Principle and intellectual honesty, we can honestly answer the question from the previous chapter – Is what the black community doing working?

The answer is factually, no. The statistics and various measurements from the same chapter prove that unequivocally.

The real question is why. And it is here there are two (very) general theories as to why black men suffer the lower standards of living they do:

Discrimination and Laziness.

Discrimination is the "politically correct" version that *everybody* offers. Politicians, journalists, mechanics, news anchors, lawyers, bankers, Eskimos, parakeet trainers, World of Warcraft enthusiasts, Fredricks of Hollywood lingerie models, Democrats, Republicans, Whigs, salsa dancers, tennis players, astronauts, cartoonists, homebrew hobbyists, strippers, priests, prostitutes, pastors, pilots, fluffers, magicians, bloggers, gigolos, butchers, bakers, candlestick makers, **EVERYBODY** subscribes to and supports the discrimination argument.

However, the reason why *everybody* subscribes to the discrimination argument is because it's the only argument that is publicly acceptable. And if you ever dared to support an argument aside from "discrimination" you are immediately branded a racist (or a bigot) and ostracized from society potentially losing your career, your education, your friends, etc. Because of this fear, nobody speaks their mind and "everybody agrees" that it is "discrimination."

It's not until you get behind closed doors do you hear what people really think and alternative theories as to why black men have lower standards of living. And what you suspect is about 60% true. Many people (and not just white males, and not just "Republicans" mind you) believe laziness or a lack of work ethic on the part of black men is to blame. But usually it is not "pure laziness." There are elements of other explanations and theories mixed in as well. Poor family upbringing, single parenthood, lack of interest in school, genetic differences, the list is endless. But "generally" speaking a large percentage of the population believes laziness is at least a component.

The problem is that neither "discrimination" nor "laziness" are the real reasons black men suffer the lower standards of living they do. Yes, elements of both arguments may describe SOME of the disparities between black and white males standards of living, but both are horribly off the mark when it comes to adhering to The Reality Principle. And if we want to escape poverty we are going to have to accurately diagnose its true cause.

An Alternative Explanation

In all intellectual honesty I cannot say that this is the 100%, verifiable truth as to why black men suffer lower standards of living. It is my best guess based on empirical data, years of economic research, political analysis, and an adherence to intellectual honesty. However, it is my belief that even if not the true cause of black male poverty, it should be 96% close enough that The Reality Principle should still be in effect. Besides, it will certainly prove more effective than what is being done now.

There is no doubt that black men are indeed victims. However, they are not victims in terms of discrimination as much as they are the unknowing pawns of an elaborate political game. This political game is arguably one of the most evil and vile transgressions against a people as it rivals slavery in terms of the damage it has done. However, what is truly insulting and cowardly about this political game is how the politicians and people perpetuating this fraud against black men have the audacity to lie right to their faces claiming they are the black man's "best friend" and supporter.

The way they get away with it is two fold. One by hiding their ulterior motives behind good intentions. And, two, they bank on people not being smart enough to think past what is called "Stage One Thinking."

When it comes to good intentions, we are already familiar with the unforeseen disastrous consequences they can wreak. All the various government programs intended to help black families (and others) were not only ineffective in closing the gap between whites, but effectively kicked black men out of society, replacing them with a government check. The sad thing, however, is despite the utter failure of these policies and their disastrous consequences, because it was all done with "good intentions" nobody thinks to question the motives of the politicians who endorsed such actions.

It is here a healthy dose of intellectual honesty is needed.

Do you really believe the politicians who claim to be helping you care about you?

If politicians REALLY and TRULY did care about the status of black men in America they would set politics aside, look at the efficacy of their policies, realize they've been nothing but disastrous and call for their immediate end. Additionally, they would have the courage to speak bluntly, directly, and truthfully, regardless of whatever accusations of "racism" and bigotry would come their way because they would want to get to the root causes of black poverty. However, have you heard a politician argue anything but "more government money" or "more government programs" in the past 50 years?

The truth is that most politicians truly do NOT care about you and only view the black community as a voting block to secure their future political careers. And instead of doing the politically incorrect and unpopular thing by suggesting an end or abatement of government programs (thus risking their career), they CONSCIOUSLY and PURPOSEFULLY advocate more government programs because they know it buys votes. In short, and in a very literal manner, they value their careers more than the lives of 21 million American black men. But because all their actions are under the guise of "good intentions," it's all good, and they get away with it.

The second reason politicians get away with this political game is because of what is called "Stage One Thinking."

Stage One Thinking is a concept developed by the economist (and black man) Thomas Sowell. His general premise was that politicians and people usually do not think beyond the obvious and stated goals of government policy, i.e. - they fail to predict the unintended consequences. So even if a policy fails, their brains cannot get past the logic of why it should have worked. And so instead of investigating the reasons why the policy failed, they merely re-advocate the same policy because of its logic.

A perfect example is "more money for schools."

Educating children is very important in this or any other country. The better educated children are, the better jobs they can get, the more businesses they can form, and the higher standards of living we can enjoy as a country. Therefore, logic would suggest that "more money = better education."

However, this is factually WRONG. It just is not the case. There is no correlation between the amount of money spent per pupil and their standardized test scores.

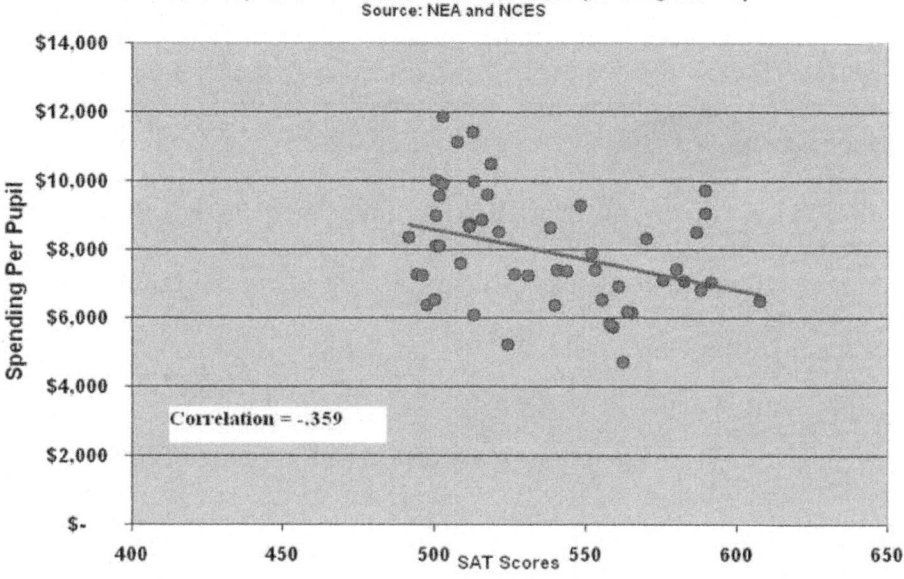

So if it isn't effective, then why do we have year after year demands that more money be spent on schools?

In part it's because the teachers unions just want higher pay without an increase in the quality of their teaching. In part it goes to pad the salaries of "administrative staff," such as counselors or food directors who do not teach, but merely collect a check for non-educational services. But the real reason schools get more and more money is because most people (including the voters) can't get beyond the "Stage One Thinking" of "more money = better schools." And so when the issue comes to the ballot box (and what politician isn't "for the children") schools get more money even though it is not going to be effective.

And it is this same inability to get past "Stage One Thinking" that provides malicious politicians the cover they need to keep up their political game, and black men under their thumb.

Understand, most people want to help blacks (most obviously, blacks themselves). Logic dictates "more government money = help for the black community." Taxpayers approve the funding, but the added money merely destroys the black community through the removal of black men from their families. However, instead of understanding the underlying economic reasons for this, most people just see the logical surface of "good intentions," and the politicians who could not care less about the damaging consequences merely advocate more of the same to get re-elected.

Admittedly, not all politicians are like this. There are some good and genuine statesmen who truly do care about the plight of blacks, they too are just unable to get past Stage One Thinking. But sadly they are far and few between.

For example, even though they are black, do you trust Jesse Jackson or Al Sharpton for a second? Do you truly believe they care about you or their fellow black man? Or do they merely profit off of being "race pimps" and "race whores," racing to a scene whenever there's an opportunity to get their faces on national TV? Or Nancy Pelosi? The woman was the daughter of the mayor of Baltimore, ensuring she never worked a day in her life. She immediately went into politics and has never left since. There's not one bill she hasn't voted for that increases the amount of government money going to the black community. But do you really think she cares about the plight of black males? Even President Obama, despite all the fan fare, does not have the traditional "black experience," benefiting from a rich grandmother and also not working a real job before immediately running for politics. Black or white, male or female, it doesn't matter. The point is if you look at the history and background of most politicians, they are typically lazy people with the money and influence to avoid real work and run for office. And if given the choice of risking that easy political career by speaking bluntly to genuinely help people, or tell them sweet lies so that they may stay in office ad infinitum, they will sell their voting block down the river because they value themselves more than the people.

But the final "brilliance" of this political game is a masterful little stroke of deception – they have a scapegoat. And a scapegoat does two very important things.

1. It obfuscates the true cause of poverty among black men (thus denying a real solution, thus keeping black men forever impoverished and thus keeping the politicians forever in office) and

2. It conveniently saves the pride and ego of black men (and others), making them loyal voters to these silver-tongued devil politicians.

And that scapegoat is white males.

You may at first disagree with this, but you have to step back, rethink things through and admit it's a bit odd the amount of political effort that goes into blaming white males for all the world's problems. White males are to blame for slavery, despite waging a war to stop it. White males are to blame for all the wars, no matter what evil they were intending to stop. White males are to blame for the wage gap. You even had people trying to blame Hurricane Katrina on a white male. But what should at least raise a yellow flag amongst the intellectually honest is a boat both black and white males find themselves in, and that is "privilege."

Since you and I are both men we automatically have "privilege." And the political implications of those that accuse us of it is that we have benefited unfairly and therefore owe them (primarily women) restitution. Of course, I being a white male have more "privilege" than you, and therefore technically I owe you restitution. But the larger point is the eeriness that comes with being accused of a crime you unknowingly, unintentionally and automatically committed merely because of the way you were born. And if you have the slightest bit of survivalist instincts within you, the hairs on the back of your neck should be standing up because the people accusing you of "privilege" have an ulterior motive that runs counter to your best interests.

Regardless, the point is that a concept like "privilege" is so outlandish and specious it proves "white males" are more of a scapegoat than they are your genuine oppressors. But also realize how predictably brilliant (and deceitful) this tactic is. Not only in providing a scapegoat does a politician protect the pride of his voting block as well as detract from the true cause of poverty in the black community, it also makes it impossible to criticize his failed policies because anybody who dares to is immediately branded a racist. Alas, this is why "discrimination" is the "official" cause of the plight of blacks and why there can be no other explanation. It also, sadly, is the reason there's been no real progress in the black community the past 50 years despite trillions in government spending.

The Ultimate Damage

The ultimate damage that comes from this conspiracy proves it is neither discrimination nor laziness holding black men down, but rather one of a self-fulfilling prophecy. Specifically, one of immobilization, defeatism, and debilitation.

Say you swallow whole what politicians tell black men:

- There are these evil, racist white males who control everything and own everything.
- On top of it, even the "good" white males are racist, but they don't know it yet because their privilege blinds them to it.
- "Evil, rich, greedy" corporations also control your life more than you do.
- You already come from a disadvantaged background, making life an uphill battle.
- And the whole game is rigged and there's NOTHING you, as an individual black man, can do about it.

So what is a black man to do?

Well, if you truly believe the situation is that helpless, a logical, rationale individual simply would not try. And why would he? If the odds are so stacked against him and the world is so bigoted and biased against him, why would any sane, self-respecting guy try?

And it is this that is the true reason for black men's lower standards of living. Not discrimination. Not laziness.

Defeatism.

Because the world is presented to young black men as a place of bigotry, unfairness, discrimination, racism, hopelessness and futility, they become debilitated, immobilized, and defeated. This, in a tragic self-fulfilling prophecy sort of way, dooms them to lower standards of living simply because they never try. They don't try as hard, because why should they? They don't work as hard, because why should they? They don't even get off the starting line because they are already brainwashed to think their lives are pointless and futile, condemning them not just to the self-fulfilling prophecy of secondary citizenship, but the psychological torture and frustration that comes from that futility.

But if you think this is evil, it gets even worse.

What is the only solution for a black man who doesn't believe he has a future or that it is within his power to change it?

Well, if it isn't in his power, then it must be in somebody else's. And by god if there isn't that same group of self-serving politicians willing to go and get other people's money for him, all in exchange for his one, measly little vote.

And this is the true evil of politicians who claim to be helping the black man.

In fooling black men into thinking that their situation is hopeless, politicians make them 100% dependent upon them ensuring their political careers forever.

Should I go work?
No, whitey won't hire you. Stay here, vote for me, I'll go get you money.

Should I go major in engineering?
No, Asians have taken up all the spots. Stay here, vote for me, I'll go get you money.

Should I start a business?
No, nobody would buy from you because "racism." Stay here, vote for me, I'll go get you money.

Naturally, the true cost of this incapacitation is the millions of lives that have been squandered over the past five decades because they were deterred from achieving their full potential. How many black doctors would there have been if politicians said, "Yes, go and do it!" instead of scare-tactic black men into apathy? How many black engineers would there have been had politicians said, "Engineering is a great way to make a good wage!" instead of disheartening them with talk of "racism" and "privilege?" It's as if you were a brand new F-22 fighter plane stuck in a hanger, condemned to sit and rot your entire life, never once allowed to fly and achieve your full potential.

The key issue is whether you're going to believe the lies politicians tell you to keep you dependent on them. Or are you going to identify them for the enemies they are to your freedom and happiness, and decide for yourself just what your capacity and potential in life will be.

Genuine Hope

I don't expect you to fully believe in my theory that it is defeatism and not discrimination that is the primary factor holding black men back. I also don't expect you to believe the more a politician claims to be your friend, the more he is your enemy. But I do expect you to at least contemplate these theories, ascertaining their veracity for yourself. However, while the picture I painted may be even MORE depressing than what you imagined the truth would be, there is some genuine hope in this dire and disgusting alternative reality. More hope than what is being presented to you "officially" by politicians, media, and others and from multiple sources you may not have thought of.

The first bit of real hope comes from the assumption that it is defeatism, not discrimination or racism that is holding you back. If you believe this assumption you'll soon have the epiphany that nobody is holding you down. All you have to do to be successful is go and do it. This realization should be incredibly liberating because it means that you are now 100% in control of your life. Not politicians. Not whitey. Not "the corporations."

You.

Naturally, this operates from a very optimistic assumption, namely that discrimination and racism do not exist...

which it does...

just not to the extent that you think it does.

The truth is that I have no way of telling you "how racist" the United States is. If you were to believe every politician you'd believe the country is 90% racist. If you believed professors and their biased studies, you'd think it's 100% racist (because everybody is racist because "privilege"). And if you looked at the comments section on some You Tube videos you'd believe America is about 273% racist. But if we were to ignore the race-pimps, politicians, biased academic studies, and internet trolls, and instead go based on experience, research, empiricism, and just a gut reaction I would say there's about 5-10% discrimination.

This is not perfect. And if you were to commit yourself fully to work and effort, there would be a 5-10% "efficiency loss" due to genuine racists you'd run into. But the point is that it is nowhere near as bad as politicians, the media and academia would have you believe. Additionally, most of the racism out there is not of the Fortune 500 variety, but Jessup the Moonshining Hick who doesn't really wield a lot of power in the country. This type of discrimination will never go away as, frankly, there will always be dumb people.

Regardless, the primary point is that your life is not fated to failure or such a huge handicap that it isn't worth trying. If you go to college and major in the right thing, you will enjoy the same success and incomes as whites. If you work hard and put in a little extra time, you will get promoted. If you keep your nose clean and stay out of trouble, you'll live a great life. There is NOTHING stopping you except the belief there's something stopping you.

The second bit of hope comes in a sort of counter-intuitive "there is no spoon" philosophy and that is:

racism doesn't matter.

As mentioned before there will always be racists and there will always be racism. It will never fully be eradicated from the world and is an unfortunate social ill we must suffer much like the common cold or tornadoes. This doesn't mean we shouldn't combat it to the extent we can, but you have to accept there will be some racism in the world no matter what.

Because of this, it's vital you learn a very important skill – know and accept what you do and do not control.

For example, I am short. This was determined not by my wishes or efforts, but between the genetics of my mother and my father. Unfortunately, being short has some disadvantages, namely in the field of attracting women. Women like taller men and this proved to be a minor hurdle in my life.

The issue is how did I respond to it?

Did I curse at the gods, lamenting my shortness?
Did I blame tall people of having "tall privilege?"
Did I demand everybody stoop so I could feel taller?

No. I just asked out all that many more girls, became a great salsa dancer, learned to be incredibly charming, and ended up with a 6'0" girlfriend who likes to wear 5-inch heels.

The point is just as I did not control my height, you did not control the color of your skin. Unfortunately for both of us, some people are going to discriminate against that anyway. It's up to us to accept this as we have no choice not to – it's out of our control. But what *IS* in our control is our ability to overcome these disadvantages.

Yes, there will be assholes and racists in the world.
Yes, they may lessen your life experience.

But if you just lie there and take it, resigning yourself to incapacitation, they win. You need to overcome them and succeed in spite of them because...frankly...there is no other choice.

In the end the choice is yours. I cannot make you believe that defeatism and corrupt politicians who use black men are the primary causes of your poverty and strife. I can only present the arguments for why that is so. It is up to you and your desire for a better life to at least entertain, analyze and think through those arguments. However, there is one compelling reason to at least consider them and that is because it costs you nothing. Nothing bad can come from you taking the time to ponder the arguments set forth above. You only stand to gain from permitting yourself to have a little bit of hope in your future.

CHAPTER 3
THE HARDEST THING YOU'LL EVER DO

Tribalism

The "Nika Riot" was a revolt in modern day Constantinople that occurred in 532 AD. It's an interesting and tragic bit of world history not because it wiped out half the city, not because it threatened the entire Eastern Roman Empire, and not because it killed tens of thousands of people, but rather because of how it started.

At the time cities would host chariot races among other competitions. Teams were distinguished by the colors they wore. There were "the reds," "the whites," "the blues," and "the greens," etc. People would cheer for their favorite color much like we cheer for our favorite teams today. However, back then (just as we do now) people would live their otherwise unnotable and boring lives vicariously through these teams, thus developing an emotional and psychological attachment to them. Thus when "their" team would lose they would become furious.

One day "the Greens" lost to "the Blues." Normally when there was a loss there was some form of rioting. However the "Green" fans were so furious not only did they attack "Blue" fans, but the entire city went into revolt. What originated as a grudge match between two sports teams, turned into a mob which then attacked and laid siege to the palace, nearly driving Justinian (the emperor) out of Constantinople. It wasn't until Justinian marshaled some soldiers to counter-attack did he regain control of the city, but not until 30,000 rioters were slain and the city destroyed.

But the really tragic thing about the Nika riot was that it was all about...

nothing.

30,000 rioters, roughly another 30,000 citizens and half a city were killed or destroyed for no damn good reason at all. A chariot race was simply lost by some guy wearing a green sash. That's it. But while this unnecessary death and destruction was ironically tragic, it does teach us a very important lesson about human psychology – tribalism.

Humans will do things that don't make a lot of sense. Riot if their team doesn't win. Get angry if somebody challenges their religion. Revolt if their political party doesn't get elected. But while it doesn't make sense on the face of it, it does when you think in terms of tribalism.

Tribalism is where your tribe or "group" is more important than anything else in the world. It's more important than other "tribes." It's more important than other people. It's even more important than reality. And so when a person puts their "tribe" (be it religion, political party, sports team, etc.) ahead of everything else it inevitably runs against reality, sanity, and other people. For example, communists believe in their economic system despite it murdering over 100 million people. College kids will riot and burn cars if their football team loses. And feminists will insist "big is beautiful" and protest if you don't agree. And while some of these things may sound delusional, if not outright immoral, it does make sense when you realize that for nearly 99.9% of human history humans survived by doing one thing and one thing only:

Being part of a tribe.

When you view tribalism through "Darwinian," "evolutionary" or survival terms it makes a lot more sense. In the caveman days your tribe was ABSOLUTELY ESSENTIAL to your survival. If you did not have a tribe or were an outcast you did not have that support structure needed to live. Predators could hunt you down easier. Other tribes could kill or enslave you. Not to mention the whole host of other societal benefits came with living with a group of people (shelters, defense, labor specialization, friendship, comradery, sex, etc.).

However, it was only until VERY RECENTLY in the 2 million years of human history that tribalism has become obsolete. Only 50 years ago heating, electricity, and power generation presented a problem to humanity. 100 years ago humans' primary concern was food. And only 200 years before that was basic civilization a standard across the world. In other words, 99.98% of the 2 million years human minds have been evolving, they have done so surviving and relying upon tribalism. And because of this tribalism is not a choice, it is one of the strongest survivalist instincts we humans have, perhaps as strong as our sexual instincts.

The problem, of course, is that society and technology have advanced so much tribalism is obsolete. We no longer have to worry about famine, we no longer have to worry about slavery, we no longer have to worry about bandits attacking during travel. And while there are still benefits to tribalism (friends, social structure, family, networking, career potential, etc.) sometimes tribalism runs counter to reality.

This puts every human in mentally stressful situations over the course of their lives. On one hand they have 2 million years of evolution SCREAMING at them to "stay within your tribe" while reality and empiricism is PROVING otherwise. And sadly, even though logically it's "simple" to understand and "just accept" reality, psychologically it is hard, even painful if it goes against the tribe.

For example consider the emphasis nearly all religions put on AVOIDING premarital sex. In the olden days this made sense to the survival of the religion (tribe). Illegitimate children are a huge drain on the tribe's limited resources. And if a girl had a child without a father the rest of the tribe would have to pick up the slack. So in nearly all religions it says you need to be married before having children.

However, enter in birth control. This technological advancement has mooted the need or purpose for such a rule. But this doesn't stop millions of good little Christian girls from fretting, worrying, and even crying over whether they should have sex or not. And it certainly doesn't stop millions of religious zealots from using this archaic rule to lord power over their congregants.

Another, more masculine example, is the visceral urge you have to kill somebody when they're driving stupidly on the road. Say you come up behind some clueless fuck not only driving slow in the left lane, but going the exact same speed as the slow car to the right of him, blocking off all the lanes of traffic. Like me you are likely cursing and swearing your head off, wishing nothing more than to ram that fucker off the road. Of course "polite" and "politically correct" people would say, "oh you don't really mean that," but the truth is, *NO deep down inside you REALLY DO want to ram that fucker off the road!*

The reason for that is again your darwinistic instincts of tribalism.

In the olden days stupid people in the tribe got you killed. So if one person was doing something particularly stupid (say spooking a herd of mammoth to stampede your village) you and the rest of the tribesmen would grab him and kill him to increase your cumulative chances of survival. But today, while ramming that slow driving fuck off the road may feel good, it does nothing to increase your "tribe's chances of survival." It will merely land you in jail.

The point is not only will your tribe run against The Reality Principle, but if you let your tribalism trump reality, there are consequences you have to pay. The trick is to have the mental fortitude to override 2 million years of evolution and instinct, and make decisions based in the real world. Because if you don't you are going to severely impair your advancement and success in life.

Your Tribe

The black community is, of course, a large and diverse group of people whose only commonality is they just happen to share the same skin pigmentation. There are native American blacks, mixed-race blacks, 100% slave-descendant blacks, African immigrants, just as there are rich blacks, poor blacks, religious blacks, atheist blacks, blacks who like Xbox and blacks who like Playstation. Because of this there is actually no "one tribe" blacks belong to. But if you are poor and wishing to escape poverty there is one tribe as a black man you are going to have to at least contend with, if not going to be part of and that is the stereotypical "ghetto culture."

The "Ghetto Culture Tribe" with its commensurate "donks," "baggy pants," designer labels, "street cred," gansta rap, etc., did not appear "out of thin air" for no reason. It is in direct response to a large and growing number of young blacks who lack a tribe of their own. This is largely the result of kicking black men out from society, replacing them with a government check, resulting in 70% of children being born out of wedlock and without a father. Without a strong father figure to lead and raise them, a baby-mama family is not strong enough of a tribe to be supportive on its own. Consequently, children go out and search for a surrogate, forming their own "tribes" with fellow children they meet at school, daycare, or their neighborhood.

For the most part people outside of the "Ghetto Culture Tribe" hate and loathe it, but what they fail to realize is that this tribe, reprehensible as they might find it, is still at least a tribe. It is at least SOMETHING for these young kids to belong to. And not only does this tribe satisfy the strong survivalist instincts one has to belong to a group, it actually does provide them a modicum of safety, security, belonging, purpose, love and friendship. Perhaps the first and only entity to do this.

Because of this either you, or people who belong to their own Ghetto Culture Tribe, are fiercely loyal to it. It is likely your single largest source of happiness, friends, meaning and purpose. Sadly, however, there is a catch 22.

For all the benefits a Ghetto Culture Tribe provides, you have to admit it is still largely formed and created by children, with little-to-no adult male guidance or leadership. Consequently, it is also short-sighted as it lacks anybody who's lived long enough to provide the wisdom about long term planning for the future. And sadly, even if there are adults providing youth within the Ghetto Culture Tribe with wisdom and guidance, chances are those same adults were raised without fathers, never escaping the Ghetto Culture Tribe themselves. This results in an infinite loop or "echo chamber" where ultimately it is fatherless children determining the rules of the tribe, and these rules most certainly run against The Reality Principle.

To be blunt and to adhere to The Reality Principle, if you look at what ghetto culture celebrates it goes beyond stupid. It's damaging and dangerous ESPECIALLY to people within the tribe. That may hurt your 2 million year strong survivalist love from tribalism, but it is reality. And this is no better highlighted than the accusation of "acting white."

For a second, step back, clear your mind, and try to approach this from a different manner.

Below are two columns. The first list are things that are largely considered to be "Acting White." In the second column are the presumed opposite, and thus, acceptable behaviors of "Acting Black."

Acting "White"	Acting "Black"
Good grades	Bad grades
AP classes	Remedial classes
Graduating	Dropping out
Going to college	Not going to college
Dressing appropriately	Pants around your ankles
Speaking correctly	Speaking slang
Respectful public behavior	Being loud and disruptive
Turn in criminals	Don't "snitch"
Obey the laws	Earn street cred

Now the reality is there is no such thing as acting "white" or acting "black" because these are behaviors all humans, regardless of race or color can exhibit. But if we were to remove the words "black" and "white" from the lists and merely look at the behaviors under the "Acting Black" column it implies blacks are

1. Stupid
2. Ignorant
3. Lazy
4. Rude
5. Disrespectful
6. Dangerous
7. Criminal

What's worse is that it isn't "whitey" accusing blacks of these traits, but members of the Ghetto Culture Tribe itself.

The question you have to ask is do you really think a tribe that accuses you of and demands from you:

1. Stupidity
2. Ignorance
3. Laziness
4. Rudeness
5. Disrespect
6. To be dangerous
and
7. To commit crimes

is in your best interests? What can you possibly expect to achieve in the long term if this is the tribe and these are the rules you are expected to obey? Driving donks is fine. Listening to rap is OK. Wearing your favorite team's jersey is perfectly alright. But to disrespect yourself so much that you are willingly stupid, lazy, ignorant, and criminal to the point you ruin your one and finite life on this planet is a personal suicide that can only be described as "outlandishly, unrivaled stupid shit."

What every young man (black or white) has to ask himself is whether he deserves better than what his current tribe is telling him he can have. And he must weigh the benefits of security, friendship, comradery, security, etc., he'd forfeit if he left his tribe against the life he'd gain joining another. But there is no doubt, out of all the tribes in all of the world, the worst one has got to be the Ghetto Culture Tribe. Whether you are aware of it or not, the ghetto culture is the most disrespected and laughed at tribe there is. Everybody, and I mean EVERYBODY mocks and ridicules it. Foreigners tell their daughters not to date black men should they attend college in America because of it. Every man I know (of all races mind you) wants nothing more than to take those fucking pants and give those punk ass kids a god damned wedgy they'd never forget. And not one man I know dreams of dating the entitled, snobby ghetto "baby mama" and all the drama that comes with it. You deserve better. You need to leave it. Otherwise your tribalism will be trumped by reality and ruin you.

The Price of ~~Admission~~ Exit

My dad was a Lutheran pastor in an extreme sect of Lutheranism called the "Wisconsin Synod." This church was more of a cult where it didn't care about its members, did not care to teach the children about Christ as much as brainwash them to become future congregants, and the teachers I endured while attending its school were mean, abusive, power-hungry control freaks that used "God" as an excuse to lord over helpless children.

Any normal, self-respecting person would flee this hostile and evil environment. However, like many cults, they employed a tactic that kept people within this tribe – hell. It was buried into our skulls at the very young age of three that if we didn't believe in some long-haired, pedophiliac-looking hippie we never met, and didn't "have him in our hearts," then we would go to hell. And in hell you would be constantly be on fire, but never die. Thus, you would suffer unimaginable physical torture forever if you didn't do what they said and think what they told you to think.

Naturally, no three year old has the mental facilities to realize it's a scam. And so for most of my (and many other's) childhoods we lived in a state of constant stress and fear, worried that if we had an errant thought or a lustful feeling we would go to hell. However, you inevitably grow up. Your brain matures, and if your environment or tribe is hostile enough, you'll have the self-respect to leave.

And that's when you pay "the price."

Understand that not only do you rely on the tribe, but the tribe relies on you. After all a tribe is nothing more than individuals, and the more individuals a tribe has, the stronger it is. Thus, when a member of the tribe wants to leave, it is a direct threat to its survival. To prevent this from happening all tribes, cults, groups, and organizations will put the errant member through roughly "seven stages of punishment." And this punishment is the price you get to pay for daring to leave your tribe and leave "ghetto culture."

Stage 1 – Dismissal

The first thing that will happen to you is that your family, friends, and other members in your tribe will simply dismiss your desires or thoughts of leaving as a temporary lapse in thinking. You'll be called "foolish" by your friends or (a common one) your family elders will simply tell you "you don't know what you're talking about." Whatever deep philosophical thoughts and concerns you have about the future of your life is simply ignored by a patronizing pat on the head. "Oh, foolish boy. Go outside and play."

The truth of the matter, however, is that they themselves are so wedded, so committed to the tribe and have known no other, that they can't possibly conceive there's another, let alone, better life out there. They know "everything," they're "always right," and they almost view your challenging the premises, rules, and foundations of the tribe as "cute," even entertaining. They really don't believe your serious and simply think it's a phase you're going through that will go away.

Stage 2 – Fear

The thing about today's tribes is you don't need their permission to take individual action. And when you start making noticeable moves to leave the tribe, they start to realize that you weren't joking. You're serious. And thus fear sets in.

Their fear originates from two sources. One, the natural fear that comes with a smaller, and thus, weaker tribe. And, two, the fear that there may actually be something better out there and that they may have wasted their lives (imagine the 45 year old corporate executive female who suddenly decides she wants kids). At this point you pose a real and genuine threat not just to their survivalist instincts, but their world view. You bring up the uncomfortable thought that their one, precious and finite life on this planet was wasted. And this then gives them the fuel and vigor to attack you and stop you.

Usually they'll recite standard doctrine or rules of the tribe that were historically used to keep people in line. In my case it was, "You'll burn in hell!!!!" In your case it may be "It's a white man's world!"

or "The Republicans will bring back slavery!" or "You're off the reservation!" But whatever they throw at you, they fail to realize you are questioning the fundamental beliefs of the tribe and previous arguments that worked in the past will not work on you now. You need to go and find out for yourself, and thus you are still not deterred.

Stage 3 – Hatred and Shaming

When it's obvious the traditional arguments no longer work, they realize you may be daring to demand a better life than what the tribe will provide you. And it is here where you really strike a blow to their egos because you are more or less telling them they're not good enough. This elicits rage.

It is a near guarantee people will yell at you,

"WHAT!!!??? YOU THINK YOU'RE BETTER THAN US!!!???
YOU THINK YOU DESERVE MORE THAN WE DO!!!!???"

And there is also no doubt you will be called every traitorous name blacks have come up with to shame anyone who dares to wish for a better life:

"You're acting white!"
"House negro!"
"Uncle Tom!"
"Uncle Ruckus!"
"Oreo!"
"You're not down with the cause!"
etc.

This will be particularly painful, not so much because of the name calling or the fact you are genuinely not a "traitor," but it will likely come from your family, friends, loved ones, and everybody else that you've had in your life until this point. What will hurt even more is when you realize they love their causes, their religion, their egos, etc., more than they love you (thankfully, not all loved ones will act this way and will respect your decision. It is here you find out who your true friends and loved ones are).

51

Stage 4 – Threats

If you do not relent their fear, anger, hatred, and envy will culminate into threats.

Threats of what?

Threats of anything.

Threats not to set foot in people's houses ever again. Threats you won't be invited to any parties. Threats not to visit certain neighborhoods. Physical threats. Cars getting keyed. Even parents "cutting you off" effectively banishing you and disowning you. Whatever they can do to either scare you or "hostage-take" you into staying in the tribe, they'll do it.

Stage 5 – Violence

If verbal threats won't do the job, some people are willing to go as far as physically punish you, even kill you. There is sadly too many stories of Ghetto Culture Tribe members beating up, even killing fellow black youths who were either "acting white" or daring to leave the tribe. These are the proverbial "crabs in the bucket" that have such miserable and worthless lives, they CANNOT allow anybody else to have better. But what is truly sick is they are so psychotic they would rather harm or kill people than see them improve their lives.

Again, I simply ask, do you deserve such a culture?

Stage 6 – Ostracization

If you didn't take the hint with actual violence and threats against your life, the tribe will finally kick you out as their ultimate punishment. You will have lost your original social network, your friends, and perhaps even some family members. They're resigned to the fact you are leaving, but they are going to make sure you can't come back, getting their last pound of flesh.

Historically, banishment or excommunication was more or less a death sentence. Thankfully, again, tribalism is obsolete and you will not starve or be kidnapped by a rival tribe. However, giving up your original tribe and all the security and social networks that came with it is still a steep price to pay. This will likely be the lowest point in your life until you rebuild your life with another tribe. Thankfully, the life you live will be better than the one you left.

<u>Stage 7 – Envy</u>

The last stage of punishment is actually not a punishment for you, but rather the tribe that raked you through the previous six stages. For as you go onto live your new life you will likely do better than your predecessors. You will have greater financial success, better romantic success, perhaps a career and a nice, intact nuclear family. Your children will love you and visit you on Christmas, and your wife will be supporting, instead of confrontational, nagging and controlling. You will by all practical means and measures have a superior life to the lives of former tribe members.

However, the true "revenge" does not come in the form of a silent envy the people you left in ghetto culture will have of you. Instead it will be that you are confirmation and proof that they were indeed wasting their lives. "Whitey" wasn't "oppressing them." "The Man" wasn't "holding them down." They were a prisoner in a cell with no bars. All they had to do was walk out, be free, and pursue a life like you did. Unfortunately, they were either too scared to leave the tribe or too lazy to put forth the effort to achieve what you did. But your presence and success will constantly remind them of this fact, as well as serve as an example to other young black men who wish to escape the ghetto giving them genuine hope and a chance at a better life.

PART II
FROM THE GROUND UP

CHAPTER 4
THE BASICS

Once you've determined you deserve a better life and are committed to the path you need to travel to achieve it, the hard part is over and the easy part begins. For there is no real secret or "magic formula" to escape poverty as much as it is commonsense, discipline, and persistence. Of course, being raised in poverty myself I have a couple tricks up my sleeve that may shorten the distance between poverty and success, but in general this endeavor is going to take time, regimen, and a religious adherence to some rules.

But before we jump into things such as education, housing, 401k's, retirement planning, etc., we are going to get a solid understanding of "the basics." These basics will provide the underlying foundation upon which you will build your financial life. They will not guarantee you riches or happiness, but they will pave the path out of poverty and make such riches and happiness much more attainable in the future. Therefore, it is vital to adhere to them, otherwise you undermine your entire financial future and success.

Don't Fuck Up

If there is one bit of advice that is more important than anything else in this entire book it is simply:

don't fuck up.

Somebody could ask you, "What's that book about!?"

and if you said, "Not to fuck up!"

you would not only be right, but would have summarized about 65% of this book.

You don't have to own a house.
You don't have to go to college and get a Masters in Chemical Engineering.
You don't have to work 80 hours a week.

All you have to do to succeed in life is merely not fuck up.

The reason "not fucking up" is so vital and so important is because in fucking up you cripple the rest of your life into the future. And not just cripple your life, but render any actions to undo your "fucking up" impossible. This condemns you to spending at least five years of your life merely getting back to square one so that you can (hopefully) start anew and still live a good life. But if you "majorly" fuck up or just "fuck up several times" you can easily ruin your whole life with no hope of recovering whatsoever.

Thankfully, the majority of people's problems today are because they fucked up. So if you simply avoid fucking up, you will already be well ahead of the vast majority of people.

There are nine major ways people fuck up their lives:

Children
Bad Company
Crime
Divorce
Debt
Housing
Stupid Degrees
Insurance
and
Taxes

And the most common and most devastating of them all is...

children.

Children

Children are, have been, and will continue to be the number one cause of poverty in the world. This is not an opinion. This is not a scare tactic. This is not what I would "like it to be." It is a fact. Children are the #1 cause of poverty.

And the reason is simple – math.

Poverty (or richness) is measured by "income per capita," "capita" meaning "head" or "individual." So for example, today the US has an income per capita of roughly $53,000 while The Democrat Republic of Congo has an income per capita of $700.

However, while everybody focuses on how much money you make, very few people ask "how many mouths does that have to feed?" And thus you can have an individual who makes $120,000 a year, but if he has *a wife and six kids*, their income per capital is only $15,000, on par with Iraq or Brazil.

Unfortunately, it is rare for an individual to make $120,000 per year. The average man only makes $43,000 in the US, so having just one child can have a drastic and immediate effect on his standards of living. But the real cost in having children is not so much financial, but rather the time required to raise them. When they are infants they need constant 24-7 coverage. This takes a toll on both the father and mother's sleep schedule, not to mention work schedule. When they are kids they need to be chauffeured to school, the dentist, summer time activities, etc. When they're older they need help with homework. And some of them never move out of the god damned house. Regardless, when you add up all the time that has to be spent raising, rearing, disciplining, and transporting kids it IS a full time job unto itself.

As if all this wasn't bad enough, you only make it infinitely worse having a kid outside of wedlock. Child support, having the ex harangue you for payment, arguing with the ex, transporting your kids, not to mention time and money spent in court. There is already a large enough time and financial burden of children to married couples, but you make it unbearable when the mother and father are separated and at each others' throats.

Unfortunately, this basic math does not seem to get through to the black community with now a full 72% of children being born outside of marriage. Worse still, teen pregnancy is most prevalent among black females, ensuring their lives are fucked up good and early with no hope for college, a career, a husband, or a future. However, there is some good news if we were to adhere to The Reality Principle. If this one, simple thing were to be changed there would be more improvement in the black community overnight than there has been under 50 years of government programs.

Regardless, the larger point is an important one for all black men as illegitimate births are such a common and crippling scourge that plagues the black community – DO NOT GET A GIRL PREGNANT. It is the absolute, #1, worst, life-crippling mistake you can make that will AT LEAST ruin you for 20 years. Put on a condom, ensure she's on the pill, even consider getting a vasectomy. Life is too short to be ruined with an unwanted kid.

<u>Bad Company</u>

I was dating a drop dead gorgeous redhead. Matter of fact, she was the hottest girl on the scene I was frequenting at the time. But as pretty as she was, she was 100%, absolutely, completely batshit insane.

This resulted in:

Temper-tantrums being thrown on busy interstates.
Vomiting up ice cream because she was bulimic
Screaming and swearing at me for failing to open doors for her
Whining about the difference between "Dayquil" and "Nyquil"
And every other imaginable sort of bipolar, pscyho-antics psycho bitches are capable of.

But the most dangerous thing she did was when she got a sad sap of a lawyer interested in her. She would use him for free dinners and drinks, and though I naively at the time believed her when she said she was just using him, in hindsight she was likely whoring herself out to him. Naturally, he viewed me as competition, and not just competition, but an inferior man. I was just a security guard at the time and he was a middle-aged lawyer. And so he became progressively aggressive in his behavior towards me in an attempt to scare me away.

Fed up with it, I sent him a rather condescending e-mail demanding we meet for lunch. I had a voice recorder and fully intended on getting him to admit he was having an affair with my girlfriend and then mail it to his wife. I was purposefully insulting, demanding he pay for the lunch, and pointing out he was old and fat. But when he finally lost it, he didn't tell me how he was banging my girlfriend at the time as much as he just physically threatened me.

It was at that point I had a very important epiphany about the whole situation – it wasn't worth it.

The psycho of a bitch that was my girlfriend and this infatuated egomaniac were bad people. And if I were to stick around nothing good would come of it. Assault, false domestic violence charges, lawsuits, perhaps even murder as emotions and hormones were running high and nobody was thinking level-headedly. A week later I dumped her and never saw either of them again.

The larger point is simply this – *bad shit* happens around *bad people*.

You yourself may be a good, upstanding, law-abiding guy. You may have no intention of committing a crime, doing drugs, or getting in a fight. But if you hang out with the wrong people you can fuck up your life real quick without you even knowing it.

A jealous ex-girlfriend claims you raped her.
Your buddy who likes to get drunk gets you in a fight at the bar.
You cousin who deals "just wants you to hold this backpack" overnight for him.

Whatever it is, one day you're about to go to a baseball game, the next you're looking at felony assault charges and prison time.

Your life is too short to be vacationing any of it in jail. It's also too short to be hanging out with bad people. Ensure you surround yourself with good, reliable, trustworthy people.

Crime

On a related note, crime is also a great way to fuck up your life.

I loved growing up in my relatively poor beginnings where the high schoolers were discussing and fully knew what crimes "would" and "would not" go on their permanent record. I found it laughable because if you were being meticulous enough to commit crimes that "would not go on your permanent record" at 17, it was almost a guarantee you WOULD commit crimes that WOULD go on your permanent record when you were 18.

Regardless, while every young boy commits some kind of misdemeanor, committing a crime as an adult is just plain stupid. The primary reason is not that you'll likely get caught or that "crime doesn't pay," but rather any criminal record is a death knell to your career and future ability to find a job. In having a criminal record you are immediately disallowed from applying to a whole host of employers, agencies, schools, and colleges. And usually they're the elite institutions of the country, preventing you from becoming "your best."

But the real risk in committing a crime is that you condemn yourself to the ghetto culture tribe forever, thereby subjecting your life to its limitations. Criminals cannot become president of the United States. Criminals usually do not become CEO's of large corporations. Heck, criminals (reformed or not) have a hard time getting qualified to purchase a home or even rent a boat. Do not cripple your life by being so stupid as to commit a crime.

Divorce

Depending on who you are divorce can either be great or horrible. If you're a woman it's typically great. You get alimony, possession of the kids, child support, half the assets, and society worships you as a "strong, independent single mom." If you're a man it's typically horrible. You get to pay alimony, you lose your kids, you pay child support, you lose half your assets, and you're immediately considered a "dead beat dad." Add to that the emotional pain and debilitation that comes from divorce and it is obvious how you can fuck up by marrying the wrong woman.

Unfortunately, it is very hard to choose the right girl and such an endeavor is beyond the scope of this chapter (but will be addressed later in the chapter on women). However, the point being for now is that if you are going to marry you MUST marry the right woman. So much depends on it. Your finances, your happiness, your freedom, your sex life, not to mention your mental health as well as the mental health of any would-be children. Take your time and choose wisely because it IS arguably the most important decision in your life.

Debt

The truth is that there are very few things in life worth going into debt for. Housing, education, and maybe a car. But beyond that the truth is there shouldn't be anything such as "credit card debt." There shouldn't be "credit counseling agencies." There shouldn't be "revolving lines of credit." And the reason isn't because sports cars aren't cool or fun. Or that it isn't nice wearing fancy clothes or having a high-end entertainment system at home. It's because the most important thing in life is other humans. And if you can not only remember that, but also learn it, incorporate it and know it, then all the material possessions in the world suddenly lose value, become irrelevant and you no longer desire them.

Sadly, most Americans prefer materialism over the love and friendship of their fellow human beings and thus, we have over $3 trillion in consumer debt. But worse, many Americans are horrible at managing their money, unable to adhere to the simple rule of "spend less than you make." Consequently, this has resulted in one million bankruptcies per year and millions more with bad credit, both of which are great ways to fuck up your life.

If you have bad credit, and especially if you file for bankruptcy, you will fuck up your life for at least seven years. It takes seven years to clear a bankruptcy from your record, and it technically stays there for all future lenders and potential employers to see. But the real way debt fucks up your life is the constant mental drain it takes on you. In being unable to refuse the temptation to spend today, but pay tomorrow, you enslave yourself to your credit card company, the car dealer, or the bank. And you're never free of them until you pay off every last cent of principle and interest you owe them. At best you'll merely be their "financial bitch" as you slowly, but religiously pay off your debts. At worst you'll miss a payment and bill collectors will harass you for your entire life. So be smart and avoid going into debt in the first place. We didn't fight the British in 1776 and the Confederacy in 1865 to free men so they could simply go and re-enslave themselves to a bank today.

Housing

While you may be thinking housing can fuck up your life if you buy one that is outside of your price range, you are correct. However, housing can fuck you up another way and that is if you buy the wrong house.

It is conventional wisdom that you should get out of renting as quickly as possible and buy a house. This "saves you rent" and allows you to "build up equity." However, that applied when you could expect to work for the same company for 30 years, allowing you to live in one house long enough to pay off the 30 year mortgage. Today not only is the labor market nowhere near as reliable as it used to be, it is also highly mobile, requiring you move to where the work is. Add to this the fact more and more work is being done via the internet and a house is no longer an asset, but a huge liability that anchors you and your finances to one place.

This doesn't mean that you will "cripple your future" buying an affordable house in a town you like. But it does throw a huge kink into any plans you have of being mobile, traveling, working abroad or being able to take advantage of opportunities anywhere in the world. Wait either until you have a very stable job in a town you like or a family you need to house before buying a house.

Stupid Degrees

If you are poor and looking to get out of poverty there is no doubt that your parents, teachers, counselors, and even the President of the United States have all told you to go to college. College was the key to escaping poverty. College was the only way you'd ever achieve anything in life. And if you didn't go to college, you'd remain a nobody and you deserved it.

However, the age old advice about attending college is precisely that

– age old. It made sense in the 1950's to go to college because very few people had degrees back then. But today EVERYBODY goes to college and now EVERYBODY has a degree. This has flooded the labor market with college graduates, driving wages down and leaving students with tremendous student loans.

However, this doesn't mean you shouldn't attend college. It means you should attend college *for the right degree*.

Sadly, most college students today listen to their teachers, guidance counselors, professors and politicians who lie right to their faces telling them to "follow their hearts and the money will follow." They do and then proceed to major in the world's most worthless shit ever.

Women's Studies
Ethnic Studies
Anthropology
Puppetry (true story)
Journalism
Theater
Zombie Studies (true story)
Music

and my all time favorite

English (even though we live in an English speaking country)

The result is one that we're all familiar with. College graduates without jobs, but $75,000 in student loans they can't pay back (not to mention the pretentious attitudes that they somehow deserve a job).

Do not fuck up your life like these people did.

Major in something useful, practical, and above all else, employable. It doesn't have to be a PhD in Nuclear Physics, but something that will land you a job. Accounting, computer programming, or the trades like plumbing or welding. We will delve into this in much greater detail in the next chapter, but just realize if you're being asked to blow $50,000 on tuition and fees, then you better damn well make your money back with the job that degree is supposed to get you in the future.

<u>Insurance</u>

Everything can be going great.
Everything can be going well.
You'll be in college getting your electrician's certification.
Maybe you even have a hottie little girlfriend that's taking care of you...
Maaaayyybeeee you have two or three little hotties also taking care of you.

Then you get hit by a truck.
Or your apartment gets robbed.
Or you run over a kid in the cross walk you didn't see.

Now what?

Well if you had insurance, you're in the clear.

If you didn't?

Well son, you're life is fucked!

Insurance, as boring as it is, and as expensive as it is (especially if you are a younger man) is an absolutely NECESSARY and VITAL expense you NEED to pay for. You simply cannot take the chance of suffering the consequences without it. And while there are many types of insurance, there are basically two you NEED to have.

Health insurance and car insurance.

Health insurance is now mandated thanks to Obamacare. You can get it either by calling up your local health insurance company or using the "insurance exchange websites" ran by your local state government. Prices vary, but for a single bachelor you can usually get it for around $175 a month.

Car insurance is also "mandatory," but Obama and the IRS are not going to hunt you down and throw your ass in jail if you don't get it. You need to get this on your own. Again, call your local insurance agent and get yourself a policy. The cheapest insurance, "liability only," depends on your location, your age, and driving record, but usually you can get it for around $125 a month.

There are other types of insurance, but the point is to imagine your life without these two vital types of insurance. If you have appendicitis and need an emergency surgery, the hospital bill will run about $25,000 without insurance. What happens if you hit a kid while driving without insurance and the family sues you for $2.7 million? Frankly, you're life is over. And it doesn't have to be an "emergency surgery" or "vehicular homicide." In today's sue-happy society, I was sued for $120,000 JUST FOR A FENDER BENDER. Regardless, the point is it may be an annoying (and even painful) cost to your budget, but without it all it takes is one medical problem or an unintentional auto accident and your life is ruined forever.

Taxes

The final way you can seriously fuck up your life is by not paying your taxes. And not only "not pay," but "fail to file" your taxes.

Naturally, nobody likes paying taxes. Because of this people have a natural aversion to doing so. But understand this and understand this well – the IRS WILL get its money. And if you don't get the IRS its money, they will come after you.

The real problem with the IRS and not paying your taxes, however, is not so much that the "IRS will come after you" like the mafia. It's all the ancillary and secondary costs associated with being audited, fined, and potentially sued by the IRS.

First, there are the fees. You already owe the IRS their taxes due. But if you don't pay (or file on time) the fees can add up rapidly. This only adds unnecessary additional expense on an expense you had to pay anyway.

Second, there are your financial records. If you get audited by the IRS and are in arrears, it will go on your credit report and this can adversely affect you chances of getting a job as well as qualifying for a loan. Doesn't matter if you're right, once it gets on your records it's a black mark against you going into the future.

Third, lost time. Dealing with the IRS is not like dealing with customer service at Best Buy. The IRS is a government agency and a shittily managed one at that. Whereas you can resolve most issues with a company over the phone in five minutes, it can take weeks or months to resolve your issues with the IRS. Lost checks, lost mail, "no, we didn't get that e-mail," "no we need the physical file," "that's not my division, you need to call this number," "why did they tell you to call this number? This is not the right department." I had one friend wait on the phone for 3 hours just to get $50.

The point is forget the money. The true cost can be the time you have to waste resolving issues simply because you were too lazy to file on time or thought you'd "cheat just a little bit."

Finally, the IRS is like herpes. It never goes away. Once you get on their radar or are flagged as a problem case, they are going to be on you like flies on shit. Just suck it up, accept this is a tax you HAVE TO PAY, pay it, and never get on their bad side in the first place.

Thankfully, the IRS typically does not audit or investigate lower income or poorer people. It simply is not worth their time. Additionally, it's not like you are going to go to jail if you make a mistake or fail to pay the right amount (unless you flagrantly and obviously engage in tax evasion). However, because of the time sink, the added fees, and the scarlet letter owing money to the IRS can have on your credit report it just isn't worth the risk to eek out a couple extra hundred dollars in savings or gamble by not filing your taxes.

Treat the IRS (and your state tax agency) like the mafia. Pay your fucking taxes.

Budgeting

If you avoid fucking up, chances are you are not going to have any unforeseen expenses. Because of this you can now budget and reliably start saving money. However, things like "budgeting" and "personal finances" are usually viewed as being boring or "stupid." That you're anal retentive if you have a budget and we all know nobody follows a budget.

Oh really?

The delicious irony I find in people who dismiss budgeting is that they are also the same people who desperately want to become rich and have a lot of money. Yet they mock and ridicule the one thing that would allow them to achieve that – budgeting.

This doesn't mean that if you simply set up a budget and follow it riches are guaranteed to ensue. But it does mean that if you wish to become rich, especially if you are starting out poor, a very good first step to achieve riches is to set up a budget.

The reason budgeting works is that it directly measures and controls the flow of the only thing that can make you rich – money. Mathematically, it's a very simple concept – spend less than you make, and over time you will accrue more and more money, in theory making you rich in the future. However, the key benefit of a budget does not come from merely throwing together a list of expenses and revenues, and saying you're going to follow it. What's key is that you *actually follow it.*

If you do that, it is amazing how much and how quickly your personal finances improve. I've seen people who were living paycheck to paycheck, with tens of thousands of dollars in debt become debt free in a matter of a year. I've seen people who never had a dime in their name, end up having $15,000 in cash in two years. And it isn't just the mere mathematical achievement of getting rid of debt and having some money in the bank. It's the financial and psychological freedom that comes from achieving these financial milestones.

Besides, the truth is simply this – budgeting is not optional. It's the only way you're going to make it out of poverty. So get ready to prepare and commit to a budget. You have no other choice.

Thankfully, while budgeting may be mandatory there are many types of budgets people can choose from. There is no one "universal budget" people "must use," and so all that matters is you choose a budget that works for you. Some people like the "envelope" budget where you put all cash you will use for each expense in their respective envelope for the month. Once the cash is gone, it's gone. You cannot spend anymore and must suffer. Some people like a "credit card limit" budget where they purposely keep low credit limits on their cards, forcing them to save. Others like to have money automatically withdrawn from their paycheck before they even see it, immediately putting savings ahead of spending. Which ever budget method you prefer to choose, however, it is vital that it is one thing and one thing only;

Thorough.

Where people goof up budgeting is they often underestimate the many and numerous expenses the average human has to pay. So while people will think of the obvious ones (such as rent, insurance, gas, food, etc.) they often forget the smaller items (such as home repair, cable, music, junk food, etc.). This leads to shortfalls in their budgeting and a failure to achieve their financial goals. However, thankfully, Microsoft has a budget template that is very thorough and is one that I used as the base model for my own personal financial budget.

You can find the template here:

http://office.microsoft.com/en-us/templates/personal-budget-worksheet-TC006206279.aspx

Or just search "Microsoft personal budget template."

Regardless of which budget type you inevitably set on, remember the key is to stick to it. This will mean having the personal discipline and resolve NOT to spend money on items you and your 2 million year-old-instinct brain desperately want, but don't need. And I would even go so far to say that it requires almost a "religious experience" where you make it a moral and philosophical point in your life to do so. But if there's one "short cut" or "cheat" that helped me keep my spending in check it was simply this.

It is women who piss away and blow money on the world's stupidest shit.

Not men.

And if you can't keep yourself from buying that latest "smart phone" or those clothes you "really don't need," then you are no different than those girls we all mock and ridicule.

You are not a girl.

You are a rock. You are a man. You do not waste your precious money on stupid shit you don't need.

Minimalism

Before you go starving yourself, wandering 40 years in the desert, trying to purge yourself like a Buddhist of all material desires, there is a much simpler and easier way to adhere to a budget. And not only is it an easier way to adhere to a budget, it is in my humble opinion the best life philosophy to live by. For not only will it allow you to stick to your budget, it will make your life much easier, much more enjoyable, and (frankly) lead you to true happiness. And that philosophy is...

Minimalism.

Minimalism, in a very abbreviated version, is where you place your time, and thus freedom above all else. You do not care about riches. You do not care about fame. You do not care about your career. And you do not care about "giving back to the community." You only care about having your time to yourself and being free.

Free to do what?

Free to do whatever you want.

This doesn't mean you're greedy, putting yourself above others, or completely clueless about finances, taking some kind of vow of poverty. But instead you work to live, not live to work. You don't work up billions like Steve Jobs did, dying tragically before he could enjoy it. You acknowledge you have one finite life on this planet, and you're going to spend as much as you can of it doing the things you want to do, not what others want you to do.

Therefore;

You're not going to slave away at the office.
You're going to work some easy, low level job your 40 hours a week and then go be a ski-bum in Colorado.

You're not going to work hard, bucking for the promotion.
You're going to work a part-time gig at home so you can spend time with your kids.

And you're not going to get that doctorate, wasting your 20's and 30's in school, and slaving away during your 40's and 50's to make your fortune.
You're going to live humbly, cheaply, and minimally, permitting you to retire at 40.

In other words, you are going to spend as little as possible so you are reliant upon having a job as little as possible, thereby freeing up the MAXIMUM amount of your life and time on this planet to enjoy it.

At this point in the philosophy you may be asking,

"But wait, I want to escape poverty! Now you're telling me to go back to it? That poverty is the key to happiness?"

And it is here that the true brilliance of minimalism lays.

Understand you only feel "poor" when you can't afford the things you want. Unfortunately, corporate America knows this and spends HUNDREDS OF BILLIONS of dollars every year in advertising ensuring you want things you can't afford. Combine this with your 2 million year old instinct that "more" usually meant survival, and you are practically psychologically compelled to

1. Always demand more
2. Be miserable if you don't have it.

But what if you were able to reprogram your brain to want less? What if you were to reprogram your mind to no longer place value on things that cost money, but value things in life that are free? If you were to do that, then you not only would be free of corporate America's marketing machine and the never-ending psychological torment of not having things that you want, but you would need less in the way of money to enjoy life.

Thankfully, you already have the answer

Other humans.

And humans are, thankfully, free.

If "don't fuck up" is the most important lesson in this book, then a very close 2nd is the lesson that "humans are the only things that matter in this world." For if you can understand that, then you will eliminate your desire for nearly all material items, thereby making you truly financially free.

But to realize this, to truly understand, comprehend and incorporate it into your core psychology isn't merely a matter of "flipping a switch." It takes a lot of serious contemplation, philosophizing, real world experience, and, sadly, age to have this epiphany. In other words, no matter how "smart" a 10 year old kid is, you're never going to convince him that spending time with his grandpa is more valuable than getting a PS4. And no matter how "wise" a 19 year old kid is, he's horny enough he'll betray a bro for a ho. But as you age and spend more time with family and friends, you'll slowly realize that playing the COD campaign solo is not as fun as blowing up your buddies online and giving them smack. Drinking at the bar by yourself isn't as fun as getting hammered with your friends at a party. And going to a movie by yourself is not as fun as going with a date. And the more you do that, doing things on your own, even if they're amazing and fantastic things, the absence and therefore supreme importance of other people will become apparent and soon you will lose your taste for material things.

Sadly, it is impossible to say when that point in time will come in your life. And hopefully explaining it above will accelerate that process. But if you set that epiphany as your goal, and make attempts to realize it, when you do achieve this realization your financial life becomes immeasurably easier as your financial desires go from the "millions" to mere "thousands."

You don't need NOR WANT a $200,000 Ferrari. You just need a $3,000 used Ford.
You don't need NOR WANT a $10,000 designer label wardrobe. You just need a pair of pants from Wal-Mart.
You don't need NOR WANT a tripped out fancy crib. You just need a safe, clean studio apartment.

All you'll ever want over life is nothing more than to converse with your friends, spend time with your wife, play with your kids, and enjoy the company of other fellow human beings. And the only real financial expenses you'll have are the ones that merely keep you alive and in good health to enjoy that for as long as possible.

Finally, there are many more benefits than mere financial freedom to pursuing a life of minimalism. In placing fellow human beings at the top of your priorities, you are by default going to meet and enjoy a better class of people. Not that there's anything wrong with materialism or pursuing a life of riches, but if you're driven by meeting new people, engaging in interesting conversation, and making new friends, you are, in turn, going to end up being a more interesting person yourself. Consequently, you will attract and hang out with much more interesting and engaging people. This will only serve to enhance your life, making it that much more enjoyable.

With better people in your life, not to mention the lack of financial stress, it is also a guarantee you are going to enjoy better psychological health than most. If you look at psychological studies as to what are the primary causes of stress (and divorce) finances are nearly always the number one answer. But in living a minimalist lifestyle you sidestep all of that. You'll likely not have a mortgage, a car you can't afford, or credit card debts impairing your finances, all grinding away at your mental health. You'll be debt free with little to worry about, your biggest concern being who you're going to hang out with later that night.

Another ancillary benefit of minimalism is how you'll be mobile and able to travel more. A perfect example is a man named "Roosh." If you don't know who Roosh is, he is an American who decided one day to throw all of his belongings into one backpack and travel the world. However, he has a specialty. He makes his living by chronicling his adventures in each country as he tries to get laid by as many women as possible in their respective towns. While this may sound like the dream job, understand ALL of his worldly possessions fits into ONE, SINGLE large backpack. If you have a house, a car, student loans, a wife, children, or any other liabilities in life, you cannot enjoy this level of freedom. A minimalist with some deodorant, boxer shorts, socks, pair of pants, and a laptop, however, can.

And finally, though ironically, you stand a better chance at being rich when you pursue and practice minimalism. At first this doesn't make sense as the whole point of being a minimalist is to not need money. But in doing so, it can actually lead to genuine riches, and the way this happens is through what is called "fuck you money."

"Fuck you money" is the amount of money required where you no longer need a job and can consequently tell your boss "fuck you." In being a minimalist you have such minimal expenses and demands for money, that if your employer even starts to give you the slightest bit of lip you can simply tell him to fuck off with no real financial consequences.

The irony, however, in having such a low threshold for "fuck you money," is that it puts you in a position of power. You don't need the money. You value your time infinitely more. Therefore, when it comes to salary or wage negotiation, you can "bluff," demanding more simply because you don't care if you get it or not. Contrast that with a guy who has three kids, has to pay child support and alimony, has a car loan, and rent he can barely afford, and that man is in absolutely no position to negotiate for more. He HAS TO take what he can get, and this then condemns him to a perpetual life of lower salaries. The result is that minimalists often end up earning a lot more, precisely and ironically because they don't need it.

The overriding point about minimalism, though, is to realize what is truly important in life. It is not money. And it is not "things." It's the finite time you have on this planet to spend with other engaging, interesting and loving human beings. And what's great about that is if you think about it, it doesn't matter how much money you have, it's how much time you have. Bill Gates has the same 74 years of life expectancy you do. He just "pissed a lot of it away" slaving away, making billions of dollars. Why not be smarter than Bill Gates? Enjoy that same 74 years of life, but not waste your youth chasing money you'll never be able to spend.

"There Is No Short Cut"

Permit me to tell you a story about two people I know.

My Vietnamese buddy

and

An angry, hate-filled, middle-aged single mom I know.

My Vietnamese buddy, like many Asians, decided to go into the sciences when he went to school. He majored in computer programming, but also delved a little bit into chemistry and computer networking. He was a nerd and was absolutely horrible with the women. He rarely had any fun in college, usually, if not always, opting to study instead of go out and party or drink. He graduated with no debt and a 3.9 GPA, and very easily spent thrice the amount of time studying than any of his liberal arts majoring counterparts.

The "Angry, Hate-Filled, Middle Aged, Single Mom I Know" (henceforth "TAHFMASMIK") did not have quite the same experience. She went to college as well, but instead of pursuing a degree in the hard sciences, she majored in English. She was (emphasis on "was") an attractive girl back then and got invited out to parties where she would drink, have fun, get laid, and return to class the next morning hung over. She took over five years to graduate, only managing a 2.5 GPA, and unfortunately had over $40,000 in student loans upon graduation.

Still, if we stop the story at this moment in time it seems that my Vietnamese friend did college the "hard way," while TAHFMASMIK did it the "easy way." My Vietnamese friend worked easily three times as hard as TAHFMASMIK, had nowhere near as much fun, and I imagine probably didn't even get laid while attending college. Yet, both of them graduated from college, albeit TAHFMASMIK had a little bit of college debt, and it makes one wonder why my Vietnamese friend (let alone anybody) would choose "the hard way" when there was a much easier (and more fun) way to choose from.

But if we fast forward to today, things look a little different.

Today my Vietnamese buddy is a senior manager at a large corporation where he earns easily over six figures. The past 20 years since graduating from college he was only unemployed three months at one time and that was during the depths of The Great Recession. He owns two motorcycles, one for speed, one for long distance. And he also owns his house outright, paying it off just two years ago. He is in no rush to get married, but I have yet to see him without a girl on his arm when we meet in public.

TAHFMASMIK, has not been so fortunate. Continuing her partying ways she proceeded to get pregnant shortly after college. This prompted a marriage that was doomed to fail, but not without first bringing another child into the picture. She never used her English degree...except...well...when speaking English, but never held a job that ever paid more than $10/hour. After her divorce she relied on alimony and child support to pay for her house, which promptly went into foreclose once her children turned 18 and her ex no longer had to pay her child support. She is now a grandmother with her child also having an illegitimate child, and I see her cursing on the internet occasionally, lamenting the unfairness of life and how more needs to be done for single moms.

Now ask yourself this question.

Who really did life the "hard way" and who really did it the "easy way?"

At first it seemed my Vietnamese buddy chose the "hard way" in life. He committed himself to studying hard at a hard subject. He forced himself to hit the books and postpone partying. He dedicated himself to his education at the expense of his social life. And in the end all he got was his degree.

However, that was a mere, short four years in his life. And though at the time it was "harder" than the path TAHFMASMIK chose, in the long run it was actually waaaay easier. The person who chose the hard way was TAHFMASMIK. Lured by an easy degree and a "party college life" she used her youth and looks to live it up early on. But almost immediately out of college life got really hard for her. She never had a real job, never made any real money, and totally destroyed her love and social life by forming a family that was condemned to self-destruct. Worst still, she's been living the hard life now for a full 30 years after she graduated from college. That's 30 years of pain and agony for four years of "the easy way."

The truth is the "ways" are actually reversed. When you are younger you will think the "hard way" is where you study tough subjects, work extra hours, and sacrifice your youth for a better life in the future. However, what you fail to realize is just how easy the path becomes once you get over that initial hurdle. The real "hard way" is taking the easy way out. The short cut. You think you're being clever or sly, or perhaps you're just being honest with yourself and don't want to slave away that much. But understand, in the long run you will spend more effort, stress, energy and resources just trying to get by than you would had you buckled down, hit the books, and pursued a "hard" career.

In short, it is easier to live the life of the "nerdy Asian kid," majoring in engineering, putting in the time at work than it is the life of an "aspiring rap artist" who merely "aspires," never "achieves," and is forced to work at McDonald's his entire life.

CHAPTER 5
EDUCATION

No doubt you've had it beaten into your skulls by teachers, parents, counselors, politicians, media, PSA's, news anchors, pastors, and community leaders that

the path to riches,
the way to salvation,
the highway to a better life is...

education.

Never mind what you study.
Never mind those news stories about college graduates unable to find jobs.
Never mind the $100,000 price tag of tuition.

No, you absolutely have to, have to, have to....

go to college.

For if you don't go to college there is no hope for you. You will forever be a loser, condemned to a life of poverty and strife. People won't talk to you. Society will renounce you. You won't even be able to get girls on a date, let alone wipe your own ass. Matter of fact, you might as well commit suicide right now if you don't plan on getting an education.

Naturally, the universal cacophony of people demanding you go to college is not quite that preposterous. But it is somewhat eerie how nearly ALL your community leaders, elders, and educators keep harping the same old song in unison.

"EDUCATION IS THE KEY TO SUCCESS!!!"

It makes you wonder if it really is.

Well, the truth is "yes," but with a large "but."

Yes, education is the path to a better life. Statistically speaking getting an education is one of the smartest things you can do. But education is also one of those nine major things that can fuck up your life. For when it comes to education or getting a college degree things are not so straight forward. Matter of fact, today they're outright corrupt and dangerous. So before you navigate the minefield of "higher education" you first need to know why you should get one.

Time and Wages

No matter what your teachers say.
No matter what your parents say.
No matter what you counselors, media or politicians say.

The only,

AND I MEAN ONLY

purpose of an education is

to make more money.

Now many people, especially educators and people in the education industry, will vehemently argue against this. They will claim "you can't put a price on education." Or "it isn't all about the money." But given the price they charge for a four year degree runs anywhere from $30,000 for a state school to $200,000 at an elite private school, it absolutely HAS TO BE about the money. Because if it's not, then you run the risk of ruining your financial life forever.

Additionally, understand that education is technically 100% free. All you have to do is go to the library, pick up some books, or research what you want to study on the internet. You don't need to go to college to get educated. Ergo, what you are really paying for when you go to college is that piece of paper that "proves" you are indeed educated. That is what colleges are charging $75,000 for and that is what employers are looking for. Therefore, the pursuit of higher education is ABSOLUTELY and 100% COMPLETELY an economic decision. And it's an economic decision you simply cannot afford to fuck up.

Thankfully you don't need your degree in economics to make this decision. For it boils down to one simple thing – your time.

If you didn't get it in the previous chapter, the only resource any human truly has is time. Yes, Bill Gates has billions of dollars, but he really doesn't have any more time than you do. Therefore, the real issue is what you do with your time to make your life on this planet most enjoyable. It is here, however, we face a paradox. In order to enjoy the maximum amount of your time on this planet you can't be slaving away, working for somebody else. However, in order to simply survive you need to work at least a little. And though the case was made for minimalism in the previous chapter, it is still nice to own nice things and afford yourself some luxuries. So how do we solve this problem? How do you support yourself, afford nice things, but work as little as possible? The answer is you need to make your time more valuable. You need to increase your wage.

Your wage is simply what other people are willing to pay for an hour of your time. And when it comes to making money you have a choice. Work a lot of hours at a low wage or work a few hours at a high wage. And working a few hours at a high wage is the way to go.

The real issue is whether you are willing to put in the additional work early on to boost your lifetime wage. And frankly, there should be no issue. It's not even up for debate. You are going to increase your wage and the reason why is you have no choice. An increased wage is the only way you will escape poverty and live an enjoyable life. However, there is a psychological problem or "hurdle" most people face. When presented with the costs of investing time now to increase your wage in the future, many people focus only on the effort and labor they will have to forfeit in the short term and completely fail to account for the benefits of an increased wage over the long term.

If you were, say, an 80 year old man this concern would be valid. The majority of your life has already been lived and going to med school will do nothing to boost your lifetime earnings or make your life easier. But if you're 23 and train two years to become an electrician, you increase your wages for the remaining 50 years of life expectancy. This not only increases the amount of money you make, but saves you many times more the original amount of time you invested training to become an electrician. Therefore, it's not so much a matter of opinion as it is a matter of math. You must overcome whatever psychological preferences you have towards laziness today, and commit to learning a skill or a trade that will increase your lifetime wage.

But how you increase your wage is a highly debated topic. Guidance counselors will recommend going to college. Economists will recommend getting a masters degree. Recruiters will suggest getting certifications. And HR professionals will recommend "continuing education." But through the cacophony of opinionated noise by all these ~~frauds~~ "experts" there's only one way to increase your wage.

Do something everybody wants, but...

nobody wants to do.

If there's a lie that is currently being perpetrated against young people today it's that you can "do whatever you want and the money will follow." Technically, yes, you can do whatever you want. But there is absolutely no guarantee the money will follow. Matter of fact, if you do "what you want," chances are it's something fun and enjoyable. And if it's fun and enjoyable, chances are millions of other people want to do it too. If that's the case, then who's going to pay people to do something fun when there's millions of people willing to do it for free?

No, the truth is that it doesn't matter what YOU want. It only matters what OTHER PEOPLE want because it is they who pay your wage. And if it's difficult to do on top of it, that is the sweet spot where wages are high.

For example, nearly every freaking American female wants to become a "teacher." They want to "work with children" and "change lives." When in reality that's just a lie they spew to hide their laziness. The *REAL REASON* they want to become teachers is because they don't want to work hard or do math. They want an easy job where the work is not arduous and they get summers off (this goes a long way in explaining why you probably didn't like school).

Contrast that, however, with the person who programs code for smart phones.

EVERYBODY wants smart phones.

BUT

NOBODY wants to program the operating systems by which they operate.

This is why people who program apps and operating systems for smart phones make around $150/hour and teachers average around $19/hour.

This isn't to say that you should all go out and major in computer programming or some arduous boring task, but rather to explain to you the reality and rules by which the labor market operates so that you choose a field or a career that does pay a high wage. It is also to convey to you, in no uncertain terms, that there is no easy way out. There is no short cut. In order to be successful in life, you not only need to get an education, but you need to get an education in the right thing, and usually that "right thing" is boring and tough as shit.

The Education Bubble

One of the benefits of being black is that you have a healthy dose of skepticism your white counterparts don't. Specifically, you don't always believe what the authorities tell you, especially when they say pie-in-the-sky poppycock such as "you can do anything and you'll be successful!" No clearer is this demonstrated in the world of education where millions of the world's dumbest white kids major in the world's dumbest shit.

Women's studies?
English?

Communications?
Theater?
Music Therapy?
Sociology?
Political Science?
International Relations?

Are you kidding me? Who the hell pays for that? What of genuine economic value do they produce?

The answers are "no," "nobody," and "nothing," and it shows.

If you have paid even the slightest bit of attention to the news you know that millions of young college graduates face the dire situation of graduating with thousands in student loans, with worthless degrees that do nothing to help them land a job or increase their wage. Howls and screams about "unfairness" and how "the government should do something" are abound, but in the end these kids choose outlandishly stupid degrees to pursue.

What should be concerning to you, though, is how so many "dumb white kids from the suburbs" ended up with such worthless degrees and debt. How is it with their parents and the financial resources of the suburbanite school districts did they get duped into majoring in such worthless shit? How did they get misled about the realities of the majors they were pursuing? You'll soon realize that in spite of having huge financial and educational advantages over their black, city-dwelling counterparts, these advantages still didn't save them.

They were tricked.
They were conned.
They were suckered.

There's something evil and nefarious going and it's the "Education Bubble."

Like government, "education" is often presented to the black man as not just his friend, but his only source of salvation. Your teachers "care" about you. Your guidance counselors "want what's best for you." And the school administrators will even go so far as to provide you free school lunches (with other people's money). But something funny happens once you graduate from high school and turn 18. Everyone you talk to in the education industry advocates, nay, DEMANDS you go to college, but (and here's the kicker)

now YOU get to pay for it.

From kindergarten to your senior year it was the taxpayers who paid for your education. Now that you're leaving that system, any additional education is going to be financed and paid for by you.

Naturally, you would think given how "caring" your previous educators were and "compassionate" the government is, they'd make tuition affordable. Besides, "the children are our future" after all. And so after applying to multiple schools, you are finally accepted at the local university where you are then informed a four year degree will cost you a measly...

$75,000.

Neither having the money, nor thinking, you sign on the dotted line, borrowing $75,000 you don't have. You then fork it over to the deans, administrators, professors, and chancellors of the school you are attending. You, coincidentally, are also asked to spend four years of your youth studying at this school as well. And only after you give them that egregious amount of money and 6% of your life expectancy will they give you your "key" to success – your degree.

You would think with such a large price tag, not to mention four years of your youth toiled away studying, the hard work is over. You should just be able to coast through life. You did what your elders and professional educators told you, and so it's just a matter of time before you land that $60,000 a year job with benefits and insurance.

But the jobs don't come.

Your applications are rejected.

And soon you have to start making the $800 a month payment on your student loans.

At first you'll think it's bad luck. Then you'll chalk it up to age discrimination, racism, sexism or whatever else your teachers and professors brainwashed you into thinking. Some will go so far as to blame it on George Bush or "the system maaaan." But the truth is you weren't scammed by "evil corporations," "whitey," or the "1%." You were scammed by "Big Education." You were scammed by the Education Bubble. And like the government trying to "help" the black community, it was the people you trusted the most that were your enemy.

The reality is that the education industry, be it K-12 or college, never really cared about you or the millions of children they purported to. They merely used you as an excuse to get extra money from the taxpayers while you were a child and tuition money from you when you were an adult. And why wouldn't they? It's the perfect sell!

There is nothing more important than "our precious children."
And we must make sure that their "futures" are the best they can possibly be.
Therefore, there is nothing better we can do than spend more money on their "education."
And if we brainwash kids during school that they should all go to college, then they'll spend...
an additional $65,000 in tuition at the collegiate level!

When it's all said and done, every year millions of "professors," "teachers," "administrators," "deans," "counselors" and what have you take over $1 TRILLION a year in taxpayers' and college students' monies. And not because they were going to provide $1 trillion worth of education in exchange. And not because they wanted to "help educate the future." They did it first and foremost because:

1. Teaching is an easy job and
2. It pays lots of money

At first you may find this hard to believe. Why wouldn't teachers and professors just tell you the realities of the labor market? What incentive do they have to lie to you about the employability of different degrees? Why would they knowingly force you to waste $70,000 and four years of your life on a piece of paper that is worthless?

To answer that, you have to look at what two generations before you decided to study when they were your age.

Understand your generation is NOT the first to come up with the "genius, diabolical plan" to major in an easy, worthless subject that was fun and hope to land some kind of cushy teacher or professor job. Two whole generations before you had the exact same idea. So when you were born there were already millions of people with worthless degrees flooding the labor market. The only problem with worthless degrees is what precisely do you do with them?

Well, there's only one thing you can do.

Teach.

And now you might finally see the education industry for what it truly is.

The education industry, kindergarten through college, is NOT an entity that is here to "educate our children so that they may live and lead great and productive lives in the future!" It is NOT a "place where kids become educated and well-rounded adults, capable of interacting with society in the future!" And it certainly is NOT a "training ground for our future technological and business leaders that will lead us towards a brighter and richer tomorrow!" The education industry is first and foremost a MASSIVE scam to provide employment for lazy people with worthless degrees.

The children are merely the excuse.

And now you can see why, despite whatever financial, economic, educational or sociological advantage "dumb rich white kids in the suburbs" may have had, they still IN DROVES majored in the dumbest and most worthless shit in the world. Their entire lives teachers, counselors, professors, and politicians lied to them simply to extract as much money as they could out of them via the educational system. They told them what they wanted to hear - that they could major in anything and it wouldn't matter - resulting in a boom for professors and teachers in worthless fields. And they further fleeced them by forcing them to take "pre-requisite classes" in worthless subjects (and the required textbooks), providing even more money for the previous generations of worthless-degreed individuals. The brainwashing was so bad (that if you put it in hindsight) they have the entire country thinking it should take *20 YEARS* of schooling to simply be qualified for a "normal job" in America today.

It is so obvious, but so large, that nobody sees it.

The problem is that it isn't just white kids they're targeting. Quite the opposite actually, and this is why black men must pay particular attention. For while white kids in the suburbs are tempted with careers in "sociology" or "communications," blacks (and other minorities) are specifically targeted with "hyphenated," "ethnic," or "victim" studies.

For example, take the concept of "women's studies" as a degree. It's, frankly, stupid. What is the fucking point and purpose of majoring in women's studies, let alone paying $75,000 for a degree in one? It offers no increase in your employability. It teaches you no skills. All it does is make you an angry, insufferable bitch with crippling student loans.

But before we start laughing at "women's studies" majors, what about "African-American Studies?" Is that any more employable or any less laughable?

Whatever "ethinic studies" degree you want to choose (Chicano American Studies, Gender Studies, Women's Studies, etc.), the particularly disgusting and betraying aspects of these types of degrees is that they prey on the minorities they self-proclaim to be helping. This results in a delicious, but evil irony.

You (likely) have female women's studies professors selling their worthless degrees to (and thus impoverishing) young fellow females.

You (likely) have hispanic "Latino Studies" professors selling their worthless degrees to (and thus impoverishing) young fellow Latinos.

And you (likely) have black "African American Studies" professors selling their worthless degrees to (and thus impoverishing) young fellow blacks.

It is the ultimate Uncle Tom douchebag move ever.

Therefore, in order to truly make your education an investment, an investment that pays off, it is vital you dismiss and ignore whatever psychological or emotional preferences you may have towards particular degrees and instead use reasoned arguments, logic, math and The Reality Principle when choosing your major. It is vital you ignore the brainwashing you'll receive from your "teachers," "guidance counselors," "political leaders," or "advisors." Because no matter how fun it would be for you to major in "African American Studies" or for me to major in "Xbox Playing, Motorcycling, Naked Megan Fox, Whiskey Studies" we would both be greeting each other in the unemployment line, both crippled with $70,000 in student loans.

Labor Market Reality

You likely already have a pretty good idea of what types of degrees you should be pursuing. Ones that are difficult, are hard, aren't fun, and are likely going to torpedo your social life while you study them. However, not everybody has to spend their youth becoming miserable heart surgeons or grumpy aerospace engineers for NASA. And you certainly don't have to sacrifice your social life to the extent you fear. It's just a matter of knowing your options, researching different careers, knowing a little economics, and being smart about it. If you do it right, you should be able to find an "ideal major" that is within your abilities and leads to a financially and intellectually rewarding career.

But the first thing we have to do is eliminate degrees that are just not worth it. And the most direct, mathematical way of doing that is looking at starting salaries for different majors.

The reason we look at starting salaries is because they are the mathematical reality of the labor market, the numerical economic data that shows us whether or not a degree is worthwhile. Naturally, what you suspect is true. Degrees that are difficult, require a lot of math, and have the reputation to be boring are the highest paying. Your "chemical engineers," "petroleum engineers," "electrical engineers" and "mechanical engineers." Down the pay scale a bit are degrees that still require a skill, but are not as math intense. Here you find finance degrees, accounting, economics, and other business majors. At the bottom of the list are your worthless degrees, euphemistically referred to as the "liberal arts" or "humanities." These degrees require no math at all, are not really intellectually challenging as much as they are political indoctrination, and while they may have the hottest chicks, they usually offer nothing in the way of increased salaries or genuine intellectual challenge. Here you find your "English Majors," "History Majors," "Women's Studies Majors," and other economically worthless degrees.

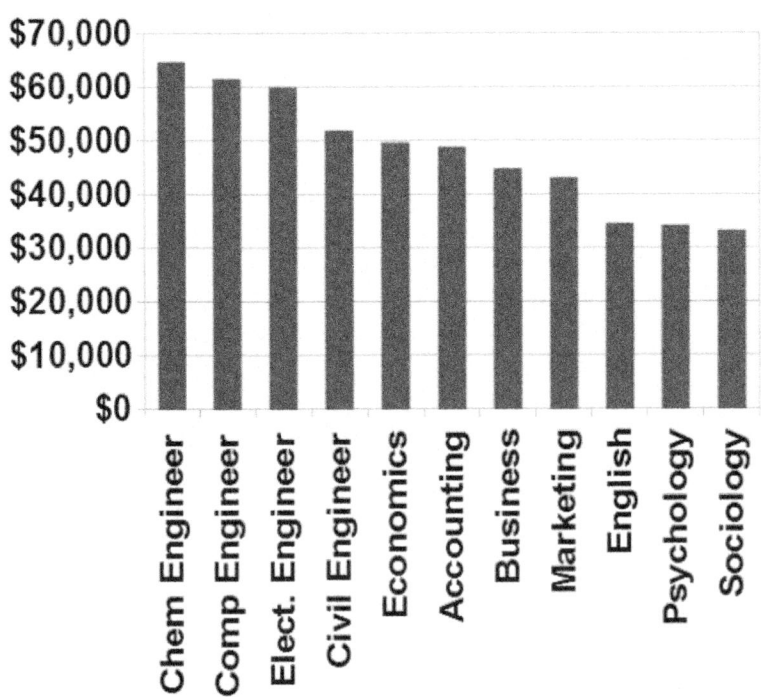

Naturally, you will want to avoid the liberal arts and lower paying degrees. However, whether you want to become an engineer or a surgeon, or would just be happy being an accountant depends on your own personal interest, as well as how "minimalist" you'd like to live. A single man with no children can easily get by on an accountant's salary. One needn't spend eight years in medical school to afford an average car and take out Chinese every Tuesday. But if you want to raise a family, live in a nicer than average home, and visit Europe annually then you may have to pursue dentistry or petroleum engineering as a profession.

Regardless of whichever quality degree you settle on, realize and accept that it is going to require rigor, math, discipline, effort, and other forms of pain. And while this may sound distasteful at first, remember that going the "easy route" is going to require infinitely more rigor, discipline, effort, and other forms of pain in your life. You have no choice. The true "path out of poverty" lies in your ability to accept this fact and capitalize on it, using it to your advantage. Not lying to yourself and "hoping" something outside your control comes in and makes your life all better.

The Trades

Cold-hearted and dire as the real world realities of the labor market may be, you may not be condemned to four years of hell, studying calculus, molar conversions, valence electron configurations, and thermal dynamics. There is an alternative. And this alternative has not only been overlooked, but often mocked and ridiculed by teachers, the education profession, and society in general. And that is "the trades."

"The Trades" or "vocations" are precise set skills that every society needs, but aren't as "glorious" as things such as being a "lawyer" or an "investment banker" or as glamorous as working for "Facebook" or "Google." They also happen to have those two vital traits that result in a higher wage:

1. Things everybody needs, but
2. Nobody wants to do.

What are these "trades?" Well they're your

Plumbers
Electricians
Mechanics
Carpenters
Welders
Pipefitters
Tailors
Chimney Sweepers
HVAC guys
Truck drivers
Farmers
Lumberjacks
Metal Workers
and other sorts of real men.

In short, they're the "Mike Rowe" sort of guys who are willing to get
dirty and make the world go around. Without them the world would
literally cease to exist and we'd all go back to the caveman days of
hunting our food in the jungle and clubbing our women and dragging
them back to our caves.

Of course today, society's "perception" of genuinely skilled
tradesmen is unappreciative. Girls don't find them sexy or
glamorous, and will usually scoff at you at the night club should you
mention you're a (GASP!) "plumber." But the truth is most
electricians and plumbers make more than your average banker.
They make more than your average "consultant." And they make
more than your average "aspiring rap artist." They may come home
dirty, but they bring home more bacon. And while they may not
wear suits or have perfectly quaffed hair, they're nicer, more honest,
and noble men than bankers, lawyers and other forms of societal
scum.

But there is an added benefit to the trades. And that is if you can
overlook whatever "society" says about the "trades," and get past the
reputation they carry, you can make a damn fine wage with a mere
one or two years of schooling.

While "Thadeus McWinthrop the III" is pursuing his triple doctorate in "Lesbian French History Salamander Unicorn 14th Century Poetry Studies" you are spending a mere two years at the local community college getting your certification to become a welder.

While "Madison McTilly Jones" has signed away her life for another $80,000 in student loans for her degree in "Hate Filled Carpet Munching Music Therapy Transgendered Studies" degree, you spent a mere single year in a computer networking program.

And while "Shaniqua Hayden-Jones-Phyllisburg" gets her fourth masters in "African American Transvestite Oppression Studies," you silently attended the two week intensive "computer programming bootcamp" and are now programming apps for smart phones from a Thai beach sipping margaritas.

And not only did it take a mere year or two to get your trade, you now make a lot more than most of the aforementioned "educated" people.

The truth about the trades is that while they're not glamorous, because they're dirty and require real work they command a much higher wage than your average college degree. Most Americans today are too proud, lazy, and spoiled to get their hands dirty, fix things, and get underneath the hood of a car. If you can do that and are willing to have a little grease under your finger nails, you can not only command a much higher wage than your average "Gender Studies Professor," but you'll spend a mere fraction of the time in school learning your trade.

Seriously consider trade/vocational school. It's the route I would have taken were I to do it all over again.

Certifications

While most of the employers in the US economy are obsessed about degrees, advanced degrees, and "continuing education," there are still some subsegments of the US economy that are more concerned with skill and ability. And instead of requiring you to jump through expensive and time-consuming hoops such as getting degrees and advanced degrees, they merely want to test you and see if you can do the fucking job. And if you can, then congratulations! You're hired! They don't give a shit if you have a degree, you merely have the skill and that's all that matters to them.

Sadly, this sort of succinct, efficient, meritocratic philosophy is only found in the IT industry of the US labor market. But if you like IT or at least are willing to pursue a career in IT this "fast track" route to a career may prove to be a compelling enough reason to pursue it.

All that's required of you is simply self-study and then passing tests to get "certified" in various skills and trades within the IT industry. CompTIA, A+, Microsoft Certified, C++, etc. etc., the list is endless. Of course this will require an inordinate amount of self-discipline, self-study, research and the ability to force discipline upon yourself. But since self-study is free (not to mention, unhindered by unnecessary and expensive "preprequisite classes") you literally can outdo your college-going peers by a speed of 4 to 1. In a single year of dedicated research and self-study, you could teach yourself more than the average computer science student will in four of university study. And instead of aiming for a "degree" you get a "certification" that is just as highly valued and appreciated by employers. Hopefully, in the end, you could be working within the IT industry at the age of 19 or 20, while your contemporaries must wait until they're 22 or 23.

Striking the Balance

While I do want to force the economic realities of education and the labor market upon you, I also do not want you to dedicate yourself to a career or study that will make you miserable. I know many people who just "had to become a surgeon." Or people whose parents "demanded they become engineers." They certainly are successful and they certainly make more money than me, but they are fantastically miserable when it comes to their careers.

Understand that you will be spending the PLURALITY of your conscious life at work. And while it is not feasible to pursue a career in a floozy field such as "Communications" or "English," pursuing a degree in a science or technological field you hate is mere torture.

Because of this it PAYS TO TAKE THE TIME TO SIT DOWN AND THINK ABOUT YOUR CAREER THOROUGHLY.

If there is a mistake humans make it is that they do not take the time to sit down and spend the time thinking, and strategically planning their lives. They're too busy making ends meet, spending time with friends, or just living life. In the end, they never spend a second steering their lives, let alone figuring out where they'd like to steer it, because they're too busy living it. In the end, 60 years later, they're not where they "thought they'd be" or "where they'd like to be" and their lives are wasted.

Because of this I am a STRONG advocate of taking the time to sit down and figure out where you'd like to go in life. And this is not a mere one or two hour investment. It takes months, if not years of living life to finally figure out what you want out of it. Therefore, there is no rush or compunction for you to decide NOW what you have to do. Yes, you need to do something to make ends meet. And yes, a one year stint in trade school, community college, or certification prep will certainly help. But before you decide to dedicate four years of your life and $75,000 in tuition to a degree or a career, it is definitely worth the time and contemplation to find a study that you jibe with and view more as a "calling" than picking a degree simply because it's "the highest paying."

You Really Can Beat the Asians

There is one final point I would like to make for all young black men out there and that is an economic, mathematical, and "Reality Principle" point. Envy or hate the "white man" all you want. The most successful class or "race" in the United States (and the world, actually) is Asian males. They make more money and enjoy higher standards of living than anyone on the planet. However, since they are a statistical minority within the US rarely is their superior economic performance pointed out or envied.

Still, we know that "Asian students" do better than every other race or class in the US be it school, SAT's, college, or career. And while many people will chalk their higher performance up to them merely being "genetically Asian," the reality is that it has nothing to do with their ethnicity or DNA as much as it has to do with the life choices they make.

To be blunt, Asian culture is superior to all other cultures. This doesn't mean Asians are a "genetically superior race," as much as it means the CHOICES Asians TEND to make are wiser and more profitable ones, giving the "false allure" that there's something "magical" about Asians. In other words, Chan is no better than you or I, he just studied harder in college. Khan is not a "genetically superior human being" to you or I, he just dedicated himself to majoring in nuclear engineering. And Minh is no smarter than you or I, he just wasn't as lazy as we were, opting to do his homework while we went and played baseball. In other words "Asian culture" is not a monopoly, solely reserved for those with Asian genetics. It's choices that ANYBODY (black, white, Portuguese, Eskimo, etc.) can make and, thusly, benefit from.

It simply boils down to the choices you make.

If all black men were to theoretically one day decide to

major in chemical engineering
study hard
ace all their classes
and dedicate themselves to a career

overnight they would have the highest standards of living in the US, trumping white males and even the Asians. It has nothing to do with your ethnicity or race. It has everything to do with your choices and determination.

CHAPTER 6
CAREER

Once you've completed whatever level of education you wish to pursue, it's time to put those nearly 20 years of schooling to use. And remember, no matter what anybody said before, it WAS all about the money.

If you chose your education wisely, things will go EASIER (not "easy") for you than others. You'll make more, have more job offers, and spend less time trying to find employment. However, the working world and labor market are COMPLETELY different beasts than anything you've experienced before. Instead of parents placating you with candy and being "BFF's" to avoid disciplining you, your boss will simply fire you. And instead of professors and teachers kissing your ass, lying to you just to collect an easy check, your supervisors will ride you, lecture you, ridicule you and make your life hell. Some of this will (hopefully) be abated if you chose a discipline where your skills are in high demand, making your employers and bosses answer more to you than you to them. But it still pays to know and understand some things about the labor market and working in the real world. Things that may prove more useful than your degree itself.

Advantages and Disadvantages of Being Black in the Labor Market

Before we get into specifics, one of the key things to do is assess your strengths and weaknesses. And while each individual will have strengths and weaknesses specific to them, black men as a group will suffer/benefit from different disadvantages/advantages as a whole. Knowing what these are will help advance your career as well as secure and protect it from any pitfalls and drawbacks.

Disadvantages

The Black Tax – While you may have every intention of working hard, majoring in an in-demand degree, scoring a high GPA, and going that extra mile in your career, unfortunately the same cannot be said for every black man.

For while there are millions of hard-working, aspiring young black men such as yourself, there are millions of black men who just plain don't give a fuck. They're perfectly happy staying in the ghetto, buying designer clothes they can't afford, earning street cred by committing crimes, "keeping it real," and running around with their pants around their ankles. In short, they live up to the stereotype, consequently besmirching the reputation of all black men. And sadly, there doesn't have to be millions of them, just a few who are then sensationalized by the media making everybody think "all young black men are like that."

Whether it's right or not.
Whether it's fair or not.
It doesn't matter.

It is what is.

Unfortunately, the behavior of these black men force all black men to pay the "Black Tax." And thus, if you wish to succeed in a career you are going to have to pay it, trying twice as hard as your white contemporaries. However, before you become disheartened or discouraged, understand it isn't and hasn't just been young black men that have had to pay a "tax" for the behavior of others.

Young people in general pay a "Youth Tax" because young people are less mature, responsible and reliable than their elders. Ergo, employers are more likely to give an older person a job, no matter how professional, reliable and hard working a younger person may be simply because that younger person's peers ruined it for him.

Women have to pay a "Female Tax" because women are more prone to file "sexual harassment complaints," bring drama to the office, and are likely to leave their jobs upon having children. Ergo, you can have the most no-nonsense, drama-free, hard working woman in the world put in an application, but her chances are harmed because of all the problems women have caused employers in the past.

We can go on, but the key thing to realize is that the world we live in is not perfect and there's no way to "snap" our fingers and make it all go away immediately. These are the rules we get to play by, and there are no other options (in the immediate future). You're just going to have to operate by that premise and work that much harder in order to prove to current and future employers that you are not like what the media, politicians, and news anchors portray black men to be, forcing them to judge you as an individual.

"The Rap/Athlete/Celebrity Trap" - If there is a sociological phenomenon that holds black men back it is the "Rap/Athlete/Celebitry/Trap." This "trap" is precisely that – a trap. A trap that ensnares young black men with the false promises of a future that will never be. However, it is not the false promises that are so alluring and tempting to young black men. It's that you can have all the riches, girls, and fame in the world *without doing any real work.*

If you look at it, all three sound fun. Who doesn't want to get paid to play basketball for a living? Who doesn't want to get paid to be a rap artist? Who doesn't want to get paid to just loaf around, nail groupies, and be a rich celebrity? The problem is the answer – nobody.

Nearly EVERY human being would LOVE to be a professional athlete, musician, or celebrity. But if EVERYBODY were successful in these endeavors, then NOBODY would be special and therefore NOBODY would be making the money they do. This results in a numbers game that has a success rate similar to winning the lottery.

Only 1 in 19,000 athletes become professionals (and not necessarily highly-paid ones at that)
Only 1 in 2,000 people become celebrities (and that includes your lowly-paid local news anchor) and
Only 1 in 10,000 musicians "make it" (rap/hiphop artists having even lower chances of success)

But what makes matters worse is that both the culture and black celebrityship blinds young black men to these impossible statistics. Nearly every role model in the black community is NOT

Walter E. Williams,

Thomas Sowell, or
Herman Cain,

But:

Some rap artist,
Fabricated celebrity, or
Basketball player.

Worse still, you combine the allure of "fame and fortune" with the social pressures against "acting white" or "studying hard in school" and you practically condemn young black men to choose from these statistically impossible careers. And once that's done, "The Rap/Athlete/Celebrity Trap" has been sprung. Corporations, sports franchises, and fashion companies successfully got you to spend hundreds of billions of dollars on their products, while also tricking you into throwing away your future life and career as you vainly attempt to pursue an impossible dream of becoming a "rap artist" or a "professional football player."

The key is to acknowledge and accept the statistical reality that we all can't become LeBron James, Snoop Dog, or the Kardashians. But we CAN all become engineers, doctors, welders, authors, electricians, mechanics, businessmen, etc. And while not as glamorous or high paying, they certainly pay more than the average "aspiring rap artist," a college footballer who didn't make the draft, or the latest failed contestant on "American Idol" who didn't get a deal and whose name nobody can remember.

A Slave to the Ghetto – One of the more appalling clients I had was a young black man who lived with his mother in New York. It wasn't that he was personally appalling, but rather his situation. He had turned 18 and desperately wished to leave New York City and live on his own. However, his mother was completely dependent upon him and his younger siblings as the more children she could claim as dependents, the more government money she could receive. WIC, EBT, welfare, public housing, you name it, she was collecting it all because of her children. However, if my client were to leave his mother, daring to live a life of his own, she (and the rest of the family) would view him as a traitor as they would qualify for less government money. His mother held this over his head as a mighty weight of guilt for daring to leave the family.

Another client I had was a young Hispanic man, also from New York. He too faced a similar situation. However, his primary concern was not so much that his family would lose out on government benefits should he pursue his dreams, but rather lived in fear that the world outside of New York was full of racists and bigots. So afraid was he of "racism" that (up until that time) had opted to stay in New York City rather than take his chances on the outside.

Both stories are sad and for multiple reasons. One, the obvious abuse of a mother or family to hold a young man hostage solely for the sake of collecting more government money. Two, the prohibiting a young man from pursuing his dreams, forcing him to stay in an environment when he cannot reach his full potential. But the worst, three, New York City fucking sucks. It's a leftist shithole with no jobs, no hope, and no opportunity for young people.

There are many sociological, psychological, familial and political reasons young black men stay in the ghetto. Some are evil such as a mother abusing you to get more government money. Others are political where politicians paint the outside world as one of hate, bigotry, and racism (thereby keeping their voting bloc in their precinct). And others are out of naivety where you just don't know any better. But no matter what the reason, if you relegate yourself to the ghetto you are purposely limiting yourself, your career, and your life long income.

And this is not a phenomenon reserved for black people. The town of Amery, Wisconsin (where I attended high school) is still filled, 20 years later, with the same redneck, hick scum that never left the trailer park in the first place. Amery may not have skyscrapers. It may not have a subway. And it may only have 2,500 people. But it is a ghetto none-the-less with all the rural amenities of teenage pregnancies, deadbeat dads who can't afford child support, meth addicts, welfare recipients, alcoholics, government housing, and early 90's pick-up trucks ("The Redneck's Donk").

The point is that this is not 1956 anymore where you can work for the local plant for 30 years and retire with a gold watch and a pension. To be successful in a career you need to be willing to move. You need to be willing to be mobile. You need to be willing to go where the work is. And the ghetto, sadly, just does not offer the economic opportunities necessary to have a successful career. Therefore, do not condemn yourself to a self-fulfilling prophecy of seemingly racist "lower wages for minorities" by anchoring yourself to the sinking ship known as "the ghetto." You have to go to where the opportunities are, and especially so if your family views you as nothing more than a conduit to a government check.

Advantages

Affirmative Action – To redress the costs and disadvantages racism can/will/may have on minorities, various laws and regulations have been passed to give minorities in the country a "leg up" in the hopes of leveling the playing field, providing the same opportunities to minorities, ideally allowing them to achieve standards of living equal to whites and Asians. However, well-intentioned as affirmative action may be, there is an undeniable other side to this "Janus-like" coin. In giving preferential treatment to minorities you by default are being racist/sexist/discriminatory against everybody else. And while you may find this OK because you're on the receiving end of it, consider the fact you are male, and are thusly discriminated against through affirmative action when it comes to females. The truth is affirmative action is the opposite of what Martin Luther King called for, PRECISELY being "judged by the color of your skin" and NOT "the content of your character."

Because of this many people have moral qualms and issues with taking affirmative action. They want to do things truly on their own, knowing they didn't receive special treatment or needed a "leg up." They want to know they were the best and did it on their own. To that I answer...

TO HELL WITH THAT!

Take the damn money and run!

While we can certainly debate and discuss the moral ramifications and consequences of "affirmative action," it doesn't change the fact that it is a reality. That it is a law. That it is a fact. It would be like Major League Baseball authorizing the use of steroids and you refusing to take them because of some kind of moral principle or scruple. Yes, in your mind you may be "moral," but the only person you hurt is you as every other baseball player is roiding up and kicking your ass. And since this book's intention is to get you out of poverty, I'm recommending every LEGAL (not moral) way for you to achieve that.

To take advantage of affirmative action is not hard at all. Matter of fact, it's almost impossible NOT to take advantage of it because every politician, teacher, professor, school, college, employer, agency, and university is practically tripping over themselves "not to seem racist," kissing your ass, practically jamming affirmative action down your throat. You merely have to put out your hand and receive it.

The earliest opportunity you'll have to avail yourself of affirmative action will likely be in high school and college where various sorts of "advanced placement" courses or other programs (where you're allowed to get college credit while taking classes in high school) will be offered. Also, about the same time, a slew of scholarships and work-study sorts of programs will be offered to you simply because you're black. And then when you get to college, all manners of programs, scholarships, support centers, student-jobs, internships, etc. will (once again) be shoved in your face by people desperate to ~~bribe, kiss your ass~~ prove to you they're not racist. You must absolutely take advantage of whatever programs and scholarships are offered to you (as long as it, of course, advances your chosen field of study).

However, while affirmative action will certainly help in school, it really starts to help in the working world. Discrimination, "The Black Tax," and other hurdles aside, the vast majority of employers are desperate to seem politically correct, non-racist, and "part of the community." But the emphasis needs to be put on the word "seem." Because more often than not, that's all it is.

Understand governments, corporations, employers, etc., don't promote affirmative action because they're against discrimination or they "care about the plight of young black males." They do it for marketing and PR. This is why you can have a guy like Donald Sterling getting awards from the NAACP, but when behind closed doors says,

"It bothers me a lot that you want to broadcast that you're associating with black people. Do you have to?"

Or worse, President Lyndon Johnson, the man responsible for the welfare system that supposedly has helped blacks so much, say,

"I'll have those niggers voting Democratic for the next 200 years."

The key is to know precisely what is driving affirmative action – politics, marketing, PR and profit. Employers will lie to your face to get you to buy their product, be willing to work for less, but fuck you over just like everybody else. And truth be told, the more a company brags about how it "values diversity" or "aims to minimize its global warming foot print," the more I know that company would have no problems laying off thousands if it meant they could make an extra 20 cents in profit.

Regardless of the ulterior motives and reason for affirmative action, the fact is that it does exist. And while it may not be as sincere employers would have you believe, you can and will benefit from it. The trick is to find a field or an industry where they are particularly boastful about their affirmative action efforts. And this results in a list of employers who disproportionately benefit from bragging about their diversity credentials:

Government
The Military
The Police
Academia/Schools
Media/Entertainment
Large Corporations

If you look at the list above there is either a political or profit motive to hire minorities. When it comes to public sector employment (government, the military, the police, etc.) politicians will bend over backwards to hire minorities because it gets them votes. This is why you laughably see 5'4", 110 pound women as cops or firefighters. It isn't to protect the people, it's to win votes from women.

When it comes to academia and the public schools, it is simply leftist politics that drives the desire to hire a disproportionate percentage of minorities. However, here again, politicians can point to the public schools and cite an increase in minority hiring which, again, begets votes.

The media and entertainment industries also promote diversity because they know full well minorities account for 35% of the US population, and that 35% spends lots of money. Additionally, non-whites are the fastest growing segment of the population, which only further secures their future revenues. Thus, not only does the media/entertainment industry gain loyalty from minorities by flashing their "affirmative action credentials," they also get you to part with $250 for a pair of LeBron shoes.

And finally, large corporations. Similar to the media and entertainment industry (sometimes part of it), large corporations know they need to keep their PR image up so they too can capitalize on the millions of growing minorities in the country. Never mind they'll sell you trillions in shit you don't need. Never mind they'll waste years of your life with reality TV. And never mind they'll gladly have you go bankrupt as long as you spend the money on their products. Hey, they "promoted diversity," so it's all good.

The larger point when it comes to using affirmative action as employment, is that some industries are more than willing to hire you because you are black. This doesn't mean you shouldn't pursue a career in the IT industry or a small corporation if that's what your heart desires. However, employment will come easier in some sectors of the economy than others. But if this concerns you, or you have some nagging "guilt" about potentially using the color of your skin as a means to gain employment, remember these employers were never being honest with you up front about their true motives in hiring you, and the least you can do is take advantage of them.

The Black Tax - At first this may sound counter-intuitive.

"The Black Tax is an ADVANTAGE?"

And actually it is. For while at first you will have to "overcome" the Black Tax, working twice as hard as your counterparts, once you prove to your employer/s that you are just as serious (if not, better) a worker than your white co-workers, employers will place a premium on your employment. The reason is very simple. In having a superior worker who just happens to be a minority on their team, employers kill two birds with one stone. They have a great worker AND they get to placate societal/PR demands that they not be racist, help support minorities, etc. etc.

While there are no statistics that directly speak to this about black male employment, it is very common when it comes to women in the IT industry. Desperate to shed the "sexist" reputation that the IT industry is only for men, employers are happier than punch to hire competent, female workers. Adding to these benefits is that male employees are just happy to have a female to look at occasionally! This results in women in the IT field making more money than their male counterparts who have equivalent work experience and education, and the same can be achieved for black men (one could make a cogent argument that President Obama is an anecdotal example of this, getting elected twice to our country's highest office).

The point is, for all the disadvantages that come along with the Black Tax, if you can "punch through it," disproving it to your current and potential employers, you get an effective "Black Tax Refund" of sorts. A refund that allows you to command higher salaries, faster promotions, and a more successful career.

The Real World Rules Everybody Must Play By

Life hates you. And it isn't because you're black. It's because you exist. The real world and the real life absolutely hates everybody and hates everybody equally. It wants you to fail. It wants you to suffer. And it doesn't care whether you succeed or not. Life is a cold, callous, unfair bastard and it is something you must fight daily in order to get to the next day.

Unfortunately, many minorities have been so propagandized they take life's hatred of them personally. They view life's difficulties, challenges, and unfairness as proof of racism. However, while racism and bigotry certainly may contribute to the life challenges minorities face, the fact of the matter is that life really is that difficult and accounts for the lion's share of people's problem. Ergo, when looking to improve their lot in life, minorities make a huge tactical mistake blaming life's difficulties on racism. It's like misdiagnosing a brain tumor for a cold and then treating it with chicken noodle soup – it won't work and your situation will not improve.

Now we can debate to what level racism and discrimination are responsible for black men's effective second place status in the world, and it would certainly be an interesting discussion. But since racism and discrimination are acts perpetrated upon you by other people, it is out of your control. What is under your control, however, is how you approach and operate within the "real world" of work. And it is here that knowing about the "real working world" (and just how much it spectacularly sucks) will become beneficial. Not only because it will help advance your career, but it will also provide an immense amount of much-needed sanity in what is literally an insane world.

The Economy Sucks

Despite what you may have heard on the news or what the president and politicians tell you, the economy (especially for young people) sucks. And while these statistics will certainly change over time, since The Great Recession a fundamental and (I would say) permanent deterioration in the US economy has occurred.

For example, the official unemployment rate is currently 5.8%, and though down from 10%, it is largely through part time employment and people leaving the labor force that this number has declined. Making it worse is that while we cheer an unemployment rate of 6% today, that would have been considered "recession territory" for most of the past 100 years. However, even this is optimistic as it doesn't speak to young people's employment prospects. The youth unemployment rate peaked at 17.5% and has since fallen to "only" 11% today. In other words, the job market sucks for everybody, but REALLY sucks for young men.

Worse than unemployment, however, is the "labor force participation rate." Translated into English, this means "what percentage of people who are capable of working are actually working?" While this peaked during the late 90's at 68% today it has dropped to 64% and continues to fall.

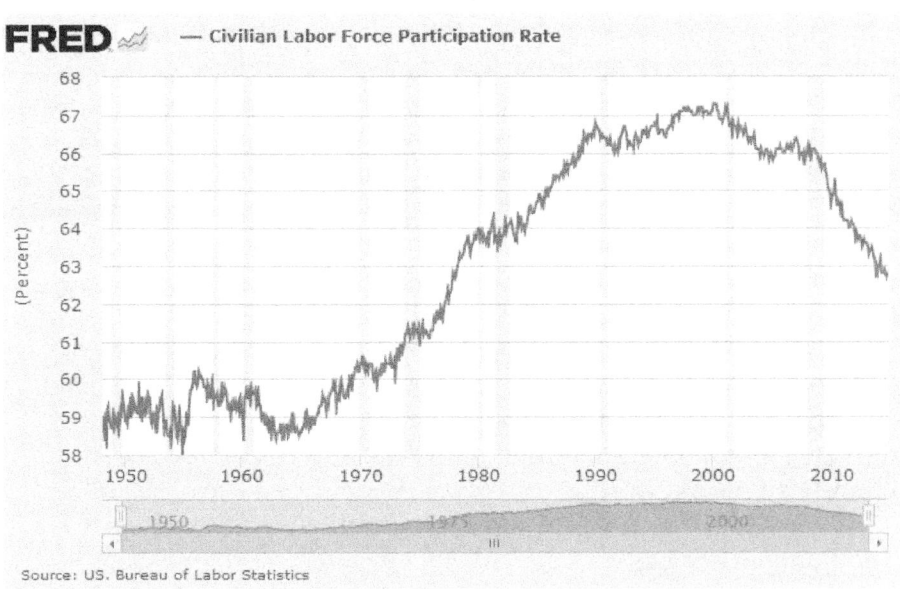

Source: US. Bureau of Labor Statistics

The reason for the drop is that the labor market is so bad, people are simply giving up looking for jobs and are instead opting to collect a government check or get by on what meager income they can scratch up underneath the table. Sadly, this is also the primary reason the unemployment rate has dropped, further emphasizing just how bad the job market is (despite the numbers).

Then there is the "*under*employment rate." People who may have jobs, but the jobs are so menial and so shitty, they are nowhere near working at their full potential and capacity. Ergo, the person who has a bachelors degree in business, but works as a barrista at the local coffee shop. While the underemployment rate is currently 12%, it is especially pronounced for younger people with an estimated underemployment rate of *50% for people in their 20's*. Thus, you could have a degree, all the credentials, and certainly be capable of more, but the jobs just aren't there. You're floor mopping skills are in more demand than whatever you went to school for.

Finally, if there is one over-arching reason for the poor career-prospects EVERY person faces in the US economy, it's that long term economic growth has been declining since the 1940's.

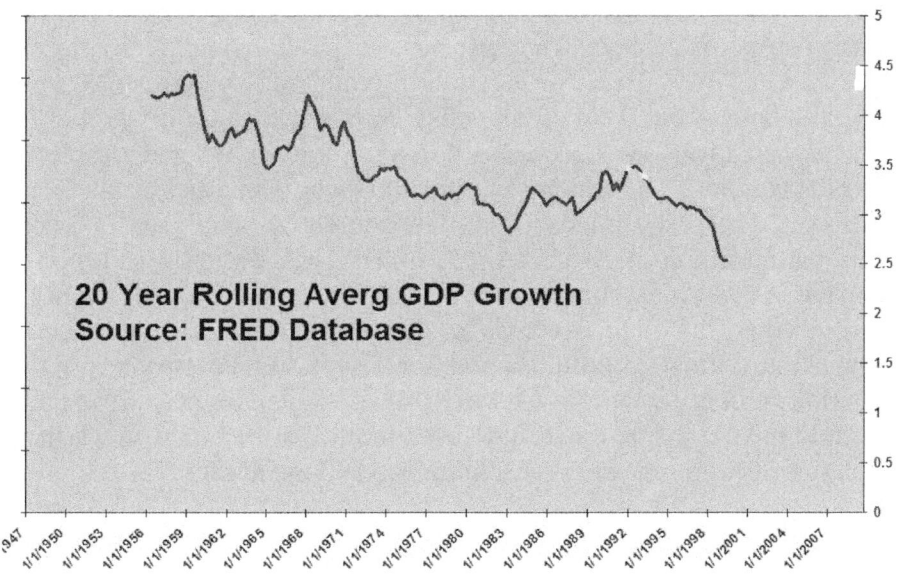

Economic growth, while originally averaging around 4.25% a year, is now just above half of that coming in at 2.5% a year. This chronic and perpetual decline in economic growth has resulted in fewer and lower-paying jobs ruining everybody's career prospects. Unfortunately, this is the economy you get to face and it does not look likely to improve in the future.

All Jobs Suck

If you think this is bad, it only gets worse. For while the labor market sucks and people are desperate for jobs, corporations and employers are acutely aware of this and they take full advantage of this fact. This has resulted in a whole host of negative drawbacks that makes it insufferable, if not nearly impossible, to establish a successful career.

First, you can expect lower pay since employers know there's always somebody else who's more desperate and willing to work for less. So not only will your starting salary be low, you can forget getting promotions and raises that keeps pace with inflation.

Second, progressive credentialism. With millions of college graduates flooding the market, employers are no longer impressed with a bachelors degree. They are now so arrogant and cocky they demand masters degrees for jobs that literally can be done with an 8th grade education. Worse, they also demand various "credentials" and "certifications" just so you can land an interview. The problem is this "arms-race" of education puts job-seekers in a very risky situation. They are forced to spend thousands of dollars and years in school and training just to STAND A CHANCE of getting a job. This means you may have to spend $100,000 in tuition and 6 years of your youth in college to "maybe" get an *interview*. Naturally, many (if not, most) people fail and are now in the disastrous situation of being unemployed with tons in student debt. In the end, it would have been better if they just started working at Wal-Mart fresh out of high school, never attending college at all.

Third, corporate sadism.

You ever wonder why the hottest women tend to be the most insufferable bitches?

It's because they can be.

Because if you don't treat them "juuuuust right," kissing their ass, bowing to every demand, there is a desperate, richer man hungry for her pussy that will. This affords beautiful women their insufferable personalities.

And employers today are no different.

Like a drop dead gorgeous girl, they have MILLIONS of desperate and hungry people begging for jobs. Therefore, not only can they demand the best, but the "mental culture" of corporate America has become as toxic as a hot night club harlot as well. Bosses are increasingly petty, lecturing and disciplining you for the minorest of offenses. Managers are insane, expecting you to train yourself, never bother them with questions, repeating the refrain, "must hit the ground running" or "I'm not here to hold your hand!" And supervisors are always reminding you that you took three extra minutes for lunch, when you're salaried and still getting the job done.

Alas, working in today's corporate environment is as mentally damaging as dating a bi-polar, spoiled brat, suburbanite princess. And like most relationships with overly-attractive women, it's not practical, it doesn't last long, it's not productive, and you leave mentally scathed when you do.

Finally, political infighting and backstabbing. To survive such a toxic environment you need to check your morals at the door and be willing (and prepared) to defend yourself against backstabbing enemies so you can advance. I've personally had people sabotage files, spend hours trying to find mistakes in my programming, filing complaints for the pettiest of offenses, and start drama where there was none. This doesn't mean you should become vindictive and malicious, harming people just to advance, but realize that is how most people DO advance in the corporate world. Be prepared to get accused of "sexual harassment," "failure to adhere to policy #124.988, Section B," using "too loud of fonts" (not joking) and other petty, childish antics you never imagined you'd face in the working world.

All Bosses Suck

From high school until I was about 30, I was under the impression that my elders, and among them, my bosses, were wise, smart people who had their shit together. That the gray haired 47 year old man was infinitely smarter and wiser than me, and therefore if he was upset or angry with me, it HAD TO BE ME who fucked up.

Not by a long shot.

Realize the majority of people who are in positions of power are also the same people to blame for the majority of the country's woes. The Dotcom Bubble, the Housing Crash, the Great Recession, the US national debt, the deficit, you name it, was not caused by young people, inexperienced in the ways of the world. They were caused by middle-aged people who were presumably "wise," "experienced," and "educated." Presidents Bush and Obama (regardless of your opinions about them) are both middle aged, both Harvard graduates, who both managed to double the national debt and mortgage our futures forever. The corporate executives at Goldman Sachs, Morgan Stanley, Merrill Lynch, and all the other Wall Street banks were not 24 year old "punk kids," but MBA-laden, gray hairs who were presumed financial geniuses that still needed you, me, and all the other regular people to bail them out. And all the "successful 50 something real estate developers" that yelled at me for "not knowing how to do my job" in the build up to the housing bubble are now either bankrupt, in jail, or both. We can go on, but the point is just because they're "older" does not mean they're wiser. Matter of fact, if they're in a position of power, it only means they knew how to play the game, sold their soul to the devil to get ahead, and are impervious to logic, reason, and principles.

Because of this, it's important to know how to interact with your bosses.

First, don't expect any logic or reason out of them. They aren't going to make decisions that make the most sense for the company or the division. They're going to make the best decisions for their career.

This often results in them asking you to do jobs that weren't part of your job description. Changing their minds constantly, never adhering to a consistent strategy, blaming their failures on you, etc. etc. Understand you are not dealing with a sane or rational person, let alone a "superior," but a flawed and (likely) failed human being who just happens to be in charge of you.

Second, because most of the relationships you're going to have with your bosses are abusive, do not take it personally. It was a tortuous 15 years constantly trying to figure out where I was failing or what I was doing wrong that I could never get along or satisfy my bosses. It wasn't until one of my bosses was called by the FBI and interrogated did I wake up and finally realize the true, inept scum most of my bosses were. However, had I known at 22 just how dysfunctional, inept, and corrupt they were, as well as I would never be able to satisfy them, then at minimum I would have been relieved of that stress and madness of trying to please them for all those years.

Realize the same thing. You can do your absolute best, they're still going to complain. Do not let it affect you, do not take it personally, just nod your head, say, "yes boss," and let it roll off your back.

Finally, sometimes bosses can get incredibly insufferable, becoming outright abusive, even criminal. Do not hesitate to go over their heads. Go to their boss and report their behavior. Of course, if you do this it is likely you'll get fired. But sometimes the gamble pays off with your boss being fired and replaced (with a slightly less-insufferable moron). Regardless, the point is that some bosses make a work environment so toxic the mental damage you incur just plain isn't worth the paycheck. So if it's come to the point you're prepared to walk and collect a government check, you got nothing left to lose in going over your boss' head and seeing if you can get him canned while keeping your job.

Adaptation

Because you are switching from an environment of schooling to employment, you are also going to have to change your mentality to deal with and survive it. And the change is going to be dramatic. In school you have teachers, counselors, and politicians all bending over backwards to kiss your ass. They're all claiming "you're the future," "children are our most precious resources," and that "you can achieve anything if you follow your dreams" They do this because that is how they make their money - the more students they have, the more money they make.

In the working world, it's reversed.

Employers want AS FEW EMPLOYEES AS POSSIBLE. Unlike the public schools, they do not have "unlimited money" being shoved in their faces by the taxpayer. They need to make a profit and to do so, they cut their expenses as much as they can. And since employees are VERY expensive, they always put employees on the chopping block. Additionally, employers do NOT like "problem employees." Whereas the public schools LOOOOOVE "problem students" or "special ed" students, they only do so because that brings more government money into the system for "special ed teachers," "guidance counselors," and all the other wimpy, timid, and disingenuous "let me be your friend and understand you" type people you likely saw in school.

Employers will just fire you.

In short, you are going from a world where people lie, but coddle you, because they live off of you, to one where they tell you the truth and use you, because they don't need you.

And you must adapt.

Lower Your Expectations

The first, and arguably the most important adaption you can make, is to lower your expectations.

In school (be it K-12 or college) teachers and professors LIED THEIR ASSES OFF to you in the hopes of you giving them good reviews, them keeping their jobs, and merely passing you along. Because of this they painted an unrealistically optimistic picture of your future.

"Follow your dreams and the money will follow!"
"You can do anything!!!!"
"You are our future!!!"

Combine that with television and media's portrayal of youth being full of parties, fame, riches, and booze, and young people are GROSSLY misled into being overly optimistic about their futures.

Unfortunately, when young people enter the real world and it isn't like an episode from The Kardashians, they get angry, upset, and feel betrayed. They think they're just having bad luck, and jump from job to job, hoping to find something that is what they were promised back in school. Sadly, that "dream job" never materializes like their teachers said it would, and that "high paying gig" never materializes like their professors said it would. And soon a great and crippling depression sets into most young people as they realize they've been lied to their entire lives.

Sadly, despite reality staring them in the face, most people hang onto their dreams because accepting this macabre and depressing reality is just too hard to take. And, thus, when trying to explain how the real world works and why people should lower their expectations, I've often been accused (violently at times) about "crushing people's dreams."

But I'm not here to crush your dreams. I'm here to tell you *your dreams never existed in the first place.* There was nothing for me to crush because *they were never going to happen.*

At first this may sound harsh, not just because it goes against what you were told all your life, but because I'm so nonchalant about it. But ask yourself a question remembering the importance of The Reality Principle:

What's crueler? People telling you pretty lies or people telling you harsh truths?

The reality is that if you lower your expectations to be in line with the real world, your decisions will be more effective and therefore, in the long run, you will have more success in life. It will also prevent (or at least mitigate) the crushing depression that is sure to ensue when you realize life is not going to become anywhere near as successful as you were led to believe. However, in this fiery and punishing epiphany will come the realization that you don't rely on "luck" or "dreams" to be happy in life, but rather things that are 100% under your control. Hard work, smart work, discipline, and basing your decisions in reality.

You may not become the next LeBron James, but you might become the next Ben Carson. And that is infinitely better than a life of moping about, feeling self-pity, because you were pursuing impossible dreams.

There is no "magic way" to lower your expectations in line with reality, but there are some key things you can do/accept that will help:

1. Your first jobs are going to suck and be low-paying. Do not expect to make a lot of money at first because not only are there desperate people in your same situation willing to work for less, there are older, more experienced people who are just as desperate. This doesn't mean you work for beans, but you go in, get the job first, and then use that as your proving grounds to demonstrate you are worth more.

2. Nobody, despite your ABILITY, is going to take you seriously until you're 35. This, again, can be considered "The Youth Tax" akin to "The Black Tax," but no matter how unfair it is, it is reality. You "may" be one of the lucky few and find a boss or an employer who identifies and capitalizes on your ability, compensating you justly, but it rarely happens. This is why (among other reasons) I recommend young people consider the military as it's about the only place that takes young people seriously and gives them a challenge in life. In the mean time, understand it is your age that will determine the level of challenge you face. Not your ability.

3. Hustle. Unless you have connections or are willing to kiss ass, the only way commoners such as you and myself get ahead are by hustling. "Hustling" is the rarest quality in the American work force. Most Americans want to come in, put in their eight hours, and then go home. But if you're willing to work that extra hour (might as well to avoid rush hour), take on that extra project, or just work a little smarter, you will start to stand out from the rest of the crowd. However, before you commit to hustle, IT HAS TO BE RECOGNIZED. I've known MANY young men and women who were desperate to prove themselves and only managed to piss off co-workers (for making them look bad), confuse bosses with superior products and ideas, and (worst) be accused of trying to be the boss. It takes a skill to find the right balance, but if you have the opportunity to hustle AND BE RECOGNIZED FOR IT, do it.

4. Nothing wrong with doing the minimum. If your employer won't let you advance or give you the opportunities needed to prove your capabilities, there's nothing wrong with coming in, clocking in, clocking out, and going home. Here minimalism and putting the focus of your life on family and friends becomes important. Because you essentially "don't live to work, you work to live." That job is a tool YOU USE to put food on the table, a roof over your head, and spending money in your pocket. You have no allegiance or loyalty to your employer, just as you have no allegiance or loyalty to a socket wrench. Of course, this assumes you don't want to advance or become a corporate executive in your career, but if you have no expectations of your job or your employers, you aren't let down when they fail to meet them.

Mentally Check Out

I have NEVER had a job where the actual job duties were as exciting as what the job description was. The job description was always a euphemistic lie told to attract more quality applicants and get them to lower their salary expectations because they thought the job would be "fun and rewarding." In reality ALL my jobs I've had in my 15 year banking career could have been done by a competent 8th grader. And that's not hyperbole or rhetoric. It's 100% true.

Filing
Faxing
Data entry
Writing
Reading

Even as a vice president at a bank, I could have done it as an 8th grader.

The problem is between college and your teacher's propaganda, your brain has likely been trained to be capable and expecting of way more in terms of intellectually rewarding challenges.

Sorry, the economic growth is just not there.

If this was the booming 1950's where economic growth was double, yes, there may be enough advances and job growth that your brain and it's capacities would be called upon, challenged, and used. But today the demand just isn't there. The tasks most people are called upon in the corporate world are mundane boring tasks that have yet to be done by computers. Filing, faxing, data entry, etc., constitute the majority of work until you get into the executive level.

This presents a paradox (and also a tragedy). All the studying, effort, schooling, and resources that were poured into your brain were for naught. You have the capacity to do great things, just not the calling. Unfortunately, no matter how tragic, we have to ask ourselves "What is reality? What is the Reality Principle?"

Well, reality is that you just are going to have to mentally check out.

For example, arguably my most successful and longest stint as an employee was when I was the "Chief Credit Analyst." A grandiose title with a grandiose job description. But like all jobs in the history of jobs, it was nothing more than data entry and some occasional writing. Unfortunately, I was so good at my job (as well as infinitely more savvy with technology than my bosses) that I was able to do full time work in a quarter of the time. For six hours a day I remained idle, getting most of my work done well before lunch. It was so bad, my dental hygiene improved greatly because I would use "brushing and flossing my teeth" as a "break" from the mundacity.

It wasn't until long that I couldn't take the inaction anymore. It didn't matter how menial or below my ability the job was, I started volunteering for whatever jobs were available. Soon I was doing the shittiest, lowest-ranked work that nobody wanted to do in the office.

I was scanning in their entire file system.
Cleaning computers.
Removing staples and paper clips from files to scan.
Salting and sanding the sidewalk.

And remember, I was the "Chief Credit Analyst."

However, no matter how degrading this situation was, this time it didn't matter. Unlike previous jobs where I would get pissed they couldn't keep up, or the work was beneath me, I had finally come to realize that no employers were competent enough at delivering enough real work to ever keep me occupied. Ever. And so I might as well do something other than looking at a blank screen for six hours a day or floss my teeth.

At this point I mentally "checked out." I realized it didn't matter if I was doing advanced "statistical analysis" of our loan portfolio or feeding files into the scanner. It was all work, it was all the same, one way or the other, and that all jobs would be like this. The only thing that really propelled me in my career were my job titles and my age, nothing of which had anything to do with ability, skill, or potential.

And it is here you must do the same.

It will be rare a job or an employer will ever use your mental facilities to their full capacity. And like bosses, you will think it's just bad luck you got this "boring job" that doesn't you use your

"Masters in Communications." You need to realize none of them will and whether you're doing secretarial work, faxing documents and alphabetizing files, or doing real work like programming models, it doesn't matter. You're still not at home enjoying life. Ultimately, work is work, no matter what you're doing, and you might as well check out mentally because not only is it the best way to do it, but it's the best way to hold onto a job, even establish a career.

Conformance, Not Performance

To advance in "most" working environments you must understand your boss does not care about your performance. He only cares about your conformance. He wants you to comply. He wants you to obey.

On some level this makes sense because your boss (should) have a higher, strategic understanding of what your group or division is trying to achieve. So whereas his orders may not make a lot of sense to you, you would presume, him being the boss and all, "knows what's best."

Still, as we've seen with the deterioration in the US economy among other economic measures, most bosses, supervisors, administrators, managers, and leaders, don't really know what they're doing. They're not supermen, and they're just as prone to failure and mistakes as anybody else.

Regardless, the point isn't whether they're "right" or not. It isn't whether they're "smart" or not. It doesn't matter if you "have a better way of doing anything."

That's not your concern. You're the employee. They're the boss.

All that matters is that you do what you're told because the vast majority of bosses prefer conformance over performance. Matter of fact, that's how most bosses define "performance" - whether you conform or not.

Of course, this is going to be hard for you, especially if you're the type of guy who wants to do "his best" or "prove himself." Sadly, corporate employment is NOT the environment to display this talent or desire. Yes, you "hustle," doing more of the things you were told to do. But do NOT bring up new ideas in the corporate world. Not only will it threaten weaker bosses (intimidated by your ideas as it may show you're smarter than them and threaten their job), but ideas (especially good ones) have the tendency to make entire divisions obsolete, costing everybody their jobs.

You save your ideas and genuine performance for yourself. You save them for entrepreneurship (which will be discussed in a later chapter).

Regardless, understand to make it in the working world you do not "do your best." You "do your best doing what your boss told you to do." No matter how dumb, no matter how stupid, no matter how mundane. You merely obey and that (sadly) is how you advance in the working world.

Tricks of the Trade

With a general understanding of how the working world works (or actually, doesn't), there are a couple short, quick "tricks of the trade" I have found useful in my past or are things I would have done "had I known then what I know now." Even though not terribly deep or philosophical, they are simple things you can do that will help IMMENSELY, perhaps even more so than your actual degree or education.

Join the Military

I alluded to this before, but because there is a bigotry against young people, as well as a lack of economic growth, you are going to be hard pressed to find an employer that is rewarding or as challenging as the US military until you are about the age of 35 and considered a "real adult."

Thankfully, the US military does not care about your age and they are more than happy to give you challenging work. Matter of fact, they will subject you to a whole host and battery of tests to find out precisely what your aptitude is, ensuring you are working at your full potential. But the real benefits in joining the US military is not the fact they take you seriously, but because it more or less bridges the gap from high school/college age to that "magical age" of 35.

During your time in the military you can take advantage of a whole host of work and educational opportunities that will not only give you experience, but certifications, qualifications and degrees. Ergo, you not only can have the US military pay for your entire education (and training), but they will give you experience as well. Add to this the fact they pay for your:

Health care
Lodging
Clothing
Food
Transport
Utilities

and there really isn't a better offer to young people serious about their future.

There is of course drawbacks to the US military, namely getting killed or maimed. People may also have some moral qualms about killing people which you may be called upon to do. However, if you can overcome these issues (or realize the statistical chances of these things happening are not terribly high during peacetime), you can avail yourself of all the military has to offer.

Finally, an often unmentioned benefit of the military is early retirement. If you stay in the US military for 20 years you can collect a pension. It's not a ton of money, but enough a minimalist man could live off of. This means if you played your cards right you could:

Enter the military at 18,
Take all the training and education you can,

Staying there for 20 years earning money along the way,
Paying nothing for housing or lodging,
Saving up a ton of money,
Graduate with an engineering degree,
With experience to boot,
WITH THE REPUTATION OF BEING A VET (which is a HUGE boost when it comes to finding employment),
Replete with a pension,

all by the age of 38.

Before you've even lived half your life, you will have been able to effectively retire, with the skills, education, and reputation that is highly sought after in the working world. And just in time when people start to take you seriously. It most certainly beats slaving away at school, earning a worthless degree, going into debt, having to pay your own rent and insurance, and having jack shit in terms of a pension at the age of 38 like most non-military people do.

Strongly consider the US military.

No Commute/Location Independence

Whether you join the military or not, the point in time will come when you will get a job. And usually this job will require a commute.

Insist it doesn't.

Remember the most important thing in life is other people. And the way you enjoy other people is by spending time with them. However, even if you have the hottest wife with the world's most loving children, if you're stuck for three hours a day in traffic, your life is moot. You're spending your dwindling, finite life cursing at traffic, not with your loved ones.

To remedy this you need to aim for two things. One, try to live really close to where you work. And by "really close," I mean "walking distance." I would even advise against buying a home because it prevents you from being mobile and forces you to take jobs that are within a "reasonable driving distance" to your house. The time, stress, and transportation costs you save alone will make the extra rent worth it, and the extra time you get to spend with loved ones will make that short commute invaluable.

Two, see if you can get "location independent employment." As the baby boomer generation dies off, their stubborn, obsoleted, and outdated insistence that "if we can't see you, how do we know you're working" will die along with them. Replacing them will be more open-minded and employee-friendly policies, namely, "location independent employment." All location independent employment means is "work from your laptop." The technology has existed for nearly a decade where nearly all office work can be done from a home office, or better yet, a laptop on a beach. You simply dial in over the internet, do your work from wherever, and e-mail it to your boss. However, while this should have launched a revolution in how Americans work (eliminating commutes, eliminating the need for downtown office buildings, eliminating the need for day care, lesser divorce, etc), old and ignorant bosses have simply resisted it.

Still, things are changing where "working from home" is becoming more acceptable and common. See if you can get "location independent" work either by insisting on it or going into fields where it is common (computer networking, computer programming, web development, etc.).

Bargain for More

Most employers will low-ball you when giving you a job offer. You can certainly counter, but a fear many people have is that if they do, the job offer will be rescinded.

This is typically not the case, because they have already offered you the job and that means they want YOU. This doesn't give you carte-blanche to demand insane amounts of sums for compensation, but you can usually counter with 15% more and usually get some or all of it. Additionally, it doesn't even have to be about money. It could be having the right to telecommute, have a four day work week, maybe have your parking paid for. So do not be timid, always ask for more, even if it's just a little bit.

Walk if They Lied

All job descriptions are bullshit. But sometimes they're just outright lies. If that is the case, you walk.

One time I got an internship at Bremer Bank in St. Paul. They said I would gain experience, which would potentially put me on the path towards becoming an analyst or a banker. Excited for this being my first internship and "job" in my industry, I bought a suit, drove in early, and was prepared to blow them out of the water.

But upon my first day, the HR lady said that there had been some temporary changes and that they would really need me to file and alphabetize some papers. Being a naïve 19 year old I agreed, thinking this was a temporary condition and soon I would get to the "real work."

The real work never came.

After two weeks of driving in from Minneapolis and standing there like a schmuck with a suit on, filing and alphabetizing papers, I had enough and walked out.

You need to do the same, just don't wait two weeks like I did.

If your employer bold-face lies about the nature and realities of your work, you walk. Not only is it insulting and disrespectful to you, that is a company you don't want to work at in the first place. If they are going to lie about what you're doing eight hours a day, making your life more miserable than it already is, then just how corrupt is the whole organization? It is almost a guarantee no meaningful work or career would even be possible in such an organization. So you aren't missing out on anything if you walk off the job...and perhaps giving your ex-boss the finger on the way out.

Move to Where the Jobs Are

One thing that angers me more than anything are spoiled kids from the suburbs, who had all the advantages of life, graduate with worthless degrees, and then ask me;

"How can I make a lot of money? Where can I find a good-paying job?"

This was particularly annoying because all of 400 miles away from me was the infamous booming "Bakken Oil Field" where the Wal-Mart in Dickinson, North Dakota was paying $18 an hour.

So I would tell them;

"Well, move to North Dakota. They're hiring everybody! It's going to suck because it's cold and there isn't a lot to do out there, but you'll make a ton of money!"

And their response was enraging;

"Well, I don't want to work out in North Dakota."

I wanted to grab them by the lapels of their shirts and scream,

"SO FUCKING WHAT YOU PUSSY!!!!???? THAT'S WHERE THE FUCKING JOBS ARE!!!!"

In the olden days, real Americans would MOVE TO WHERE THE WORK WAS. They didn't sit on their asses, sipping their $7 Starbucks "Frappcino's," living off of their parents dime, while they typed away on Facebook using their fucking Apple laptops, whining about how there weren't any jobs. They said, "Shit, I need a job" and they would move to where the jobs were.

Please do not be the stereotypical whinny, spoiled brat, suburbanite, liberal arts majoring cunt. Go on the internet, find out where unemployment is low, labor is in demand, send out applications, land a job, and move there.

Always Be Applying for Jobs

The typical approach an applicant has to a job is to get one and then relax with a reliving "whew." The reason for this is that people are always desperate to find employment and that task takes work. Thus, when you finally land a job you think, "Thank god, I can relax."

No you can't.

While you may have thought you crossed the finish line, the truth is this race never ends. And it's a guarantee that you will either leave that job or they will fire you. In either case, it's usually out of duress and stress you go looking for another job, not because you think you can find a better job offer. Unfortunately, this means most people start looking for another job when they think they're going to lose their current one. This means they're job hunting from a position of desperation, not power, almost ensuring they will take "whatever they can." This results in the unenviable position of jumping from one frying pan into another and never leads to a successful career.

You need to negotiate for jobs from a position of power. You need to have multiple job offers on your plate at all times. Which means in addition to your day time job, you have a part-time job of always being on the look out for a better offer. This doesn't mean you spend 20 hours a week applying for other jobs, but you do spend a couple hours a week perusing the want ads, and if you see something you might like, you apply for it. Ideally, this constant trickle of job searching will result in you having several offers on the table that will not only allow you to ask your current employer for more, but should your employer become lippy, abusive, or dishonest, you simply walk and take up employment with his competitor. This alone is worth the extra time dedicated towards your perpetual job search as it will spare you the psychological torment and stress of being desperate to find another job before you get fired.

Sometimes You Just Weren't Cut Out for It

One of the few bits of good advice I received from a boss came at my last and final stint at banking. I had given my boss my resignation and he said, "Yeah, well I could see this coming." He was going to continue on, but so indifferent about the job and what he had to say, I was about to interrupt him and tell him, "I don't care." However, I listened and it was one of the few lectures that had some value to it. Specifically, he said;

"Look, you just aren't cut out for banking. Do something else. Find something else. Just not banking."

And he was right. The past 15 years in banking was nothing but ramming heads with management, chasing down deadbeats to pay us the money they owed us, repossessing the world's shittiest and most degraded collateral, and reading through the world's dumbest loan requests. There was not ONE bank where the work was logical, productive, efficient, or profitable. And whereas I thought it was just bad luck on my part, it was the nature of the entire banking industry. All banks were corrupt. All bankers were dumber than shit. And all they cared about was making commission, not profit.

Had I not a soul, had I the ability not to look at math and predict loans would go bad, had I the ability to not give a fuck about the shareholder, employees, and the taxpayer, I would have made a GREAT banker.

"Approve everything! Where's my commission!? Let's go golfing!"

But I couldn't do it. I insisted on lending money to quality borrowers who were likely to pay us back. And that just was not what the industry was about.

The point is that you may be great at what you do. You may actually be the best in the entire industry. But there is something about the culture or the nature of the industry that is just not compatible with you. And the question you need to ask is who is going to budge? You or the industry?

Sadly, many people have not only had to give up on their dreams, but give up on sane and reasonable careers they heavily invested in, having to restart from scratch late in life. The trick is to not get so far invested that it's too late to switch careers. You need to keep a finger on the pulse of the industry you're in as well as honestly assess yourself and whether you belong in that industry. If it's like pulling teeth just to achieve the most basic of advances in a career, it is likely you have chosen the wrong path. Not because of anything you did or failed to do, but because you and the industry are just not compatible.

The Best Career

If you hadn't noticed the "Real World Rules Everybody Must Abide By" is not terribly optimistic, hopeful, or even "neutral" about people's prospects of working in the real world. Matter of fact, it sounds downright painful. However, for all of its pessimism and cynicism, it is 100% true. Nobody likes going to work because work is not an enjoyable experience. It sucks. It's why the American dream is "early retirement," people fake calling in sick to work, and why John Goodman's "Fuck You" performance in "The Gambler" should earn him an Oscar.

But there is ONE form of employment that actually is enjoyable. And not just enjoyable, but "the" optimal form of employment.

Entrepreneurship.

For after you've suffered enough working in the real world, it will become very apparent, very quickly to every man out there that his life is just too damn short to be working for other people. And after gaining enough education, training, experience, and detestment working for other people, you'll have the ability, capacity, and drive to strike out on your own. And that is when the real fun begins.

CHAPTER 7
ENTREPRENEURSHIP

Remember everything I said in the previous chapter? Yeah, well forget it. For while working hard and having a career may get you out of the ghetto, it certainly won't make you rich. It also won't make you happy, as how can anybody be happy working under today's sadistic corporate environment? No, the truth about being rich, successful, and happy with your working life is that it can only be achieved through one thing and one thing only – entrepreneurship.

But before you jump headlong into the world of self-employment, understand it is not for everybody. Not only can "not everybody" be self employed, but most people plain do not have the mentality or psychological rigor for it. Because of this, most people are faced with a catch 22 when it comes to running their own company. They're either not capable of it, which condemns them to a life of working for somebody else, or they're still not capable of it, yet make an attempt to start their own business anyway, which only condemns them to failure. Thus, it is up to you and some serious soul searching to see if you have what it takes to become an entrepreneur. If you do, great! It's going to be a tough road, but the rewards are definitely worth it. If you're not. That's all right. There is absolutely nothing wrong with working a regular job. It's noble and millions of people live great and happy lives working regular jobs. You're just going to have to accept you will likely not be "rich," you will answer to somebody for the rest of your life, and your job is statistically very unlikely to ever be rewarding.

An Idea

If there is one thing that will determine whether you will be a successful entrepreneur or not it is whether you have a good idea. Unfortunately, most Americans are so lazy and so spoiled, they confuse "cool" ideas with "good" ideas. They confuse "ideas that people are willing to pay for" with "ideas they personally want to pursue." Ideas that will "make you rich" with ideas that will "bankrupt the hell out of you."

Nowhere was this more apparent than when I worked in banking.

Not once in 15 years did an aspiring entrepreneur approach me or my bank with a good idea. They were all ideas that were either outlandishly stupid or ideas that were done a million times over.

There was the woman of incomprehensible stupidity that wanted us to loan her $300,000 so she could open a cereal restaurant. All the "cool kids in college who miss their moms," she opined, would show up at her "cereal restaurant" in their pajamas and have breakfast. The majority of the money we would lend her would be spent on milk...which would go sour in about two weeks.

There was the woman who wanted to start her own record production company. No experience. No money. No musical talent. It was "her dream" ever since she was a child and she decided it was time to start "getting serious about it."

And then there was the never-ending line of recently-divorced, midlife-crisis men who wanted to open up a "sports bar." Never mind sports bars have a failure rate of 95%. Never mind none of these aging dude-bro-douches ever ran a bar. And never mind there's a sports bar on every fucking corner in these United States of America. Nope, all that mattered was it was these washed-up-jocks' "dream" to own a sports bar.

The point is whether it was a "Cereal Lady," a "Record Label Girl," or an army of "Sports Bar Dude-Bro-Douches," all of them committed the cardinal sin when deciding what kind of a business to start - they put what THEY WANTED TO DO ahead of what PEOPLE WERE WILLING TO PAY FOR.

When it comes to entrepreneurship the number one rule you MUST follow is to produce what other people want. Not what you'd "like to produce."

Of course, this is the trick when it comes to entrepreneurship. Ideally, you'd like to do something you enjoy AND have it be something that is also in demand. Unfortunately, most "business ideas" that fall under these two categories are considered hobbies.

Raising wiener dogs.
Running a sports bar.
Opening up a restaurant.
Operating an ice cream parlour.

All fun, but since EVERYBODY'S DOING IT, there's no profit.

Thus, this is the hardest part of entrepreneurship. Coming up with that "golden" idea that is both enjoyable, in demand, and never thought of before. What that is, however, is up for you to decide. One thing that irks me to no end in my Asshole Consulting business is when young men come up to me and ask me,

"What kind of business should I start?"

I want to find out where they live, drive there, and beat the fucking shit out of them because if I knew what kind of business they should start **THEN I WOULD START THE FUCKING BUSINESS AND KEEP ALL OF THE FUCKING MONEY MYSELF!!!**

Sadly, that is what you have to figure out. It takes time. It takes contemplation. It takes thought. And it also takes a creative mind, a keen eye, thinking outside the box, and an outlook for ideas that nobody else has thought of. However, whereas I cannot tell you specifically what kind of business to start, I can tell you some qualities and traits of businesses that tend to be more successful than others. And since it is unlikely you will be starting up the next Microsoft, requesting billions of dollars in start up money, these ideas are perfect for poor or lower-income folks (and are largely the reasons for my own personal success in business).

Low Capital Companies

"Low capital companies" is just a fancy phrase for saying, "companies that don't require a lot of money." If you are poor (like I was) you don't have millions of dollars laying around to start some massive factory. Matter of fact, if you were like me, you don't even have $10,000 in your name. This lack of money makes any entrepreneurial endeavors that required lots of cash impossible.

However, what this lack of money does do is force you to be creative and clever when it comes to coming up with business ideas.

For example, my "first technical" business was teaching dance classes. My total expenditure on equipment was $200 for a stereo, and about $50 on CD's. I certainly wasn't making millions, but I did manage to make $46,000 in one year. All for a $250 investment (and some time learning ballroom dance).

Another example, Maurice Harary. You may not have heard of Maurice Harary, but you have heard about Osama Bin Laden. Well, when Bin Laden was killed Maurice set up a website and sold "Dead Osama Bin Laden" shirts and within two days made over $100,000 in profits. Unfortunately, he was a fucking moron and later refunded people their money because he "made profits on the death of a person," but the point still remains – low capital, high profit.

And a final example is Jenna Marbles. Jenna Marbles, if you don't know who she is, is arguably the most prominent and popular You Tube celebrity there is, estimating to make over $4 million per year on her videos. All she does is merely film herself and her ramblings, posting them on the internet for all of her fans to see. But the shallow content of her videos aside, consider what it really takes to make those videos. A camera, a computer, some props, and some editing software. That's it. No more than $4,000 was spent on that business venture and she's turning it into $4 million.

Now, this doesn't mean we're all going to have my mad ballroom dancing skills, or the foresight of Maurice, or the beauty of Jenna Marbles. But if you keep your eyes open, notice trends, or just start training your brain to identify opportunities, a lot of them do not require huge sums of money and can be taken advantage of by poorer people such as ourselves, often (and easily) ending our poverty once and for all.

Scalability

Along the same lines of "low capital companies" is scalability. This is vital for any aspiring businessman because nobody is born an entrepreneur with a fully functioning and profitable business. i.e. -

everybody starts out having a daytime job that puts food on the table, and from there launches a part-time company that inevitably grows enough to replace their full-time job. Thus, unless you have a REALLY GREAT idea that is FOR SURE a winner, you can't afford to give up your day time gig to pursue your business idea. Your business idea has to start out as a part-time venture, with the ability to grow and "scale."

But it isn't just an issue of whether your company is scalable, but whether you can keep up with it. Can you keep up with the growth of your company?

For example, my company "Asshole Consulting" (another "low capital company") would get ONE request every TWO days. It was cute. I was bored when I set up the company. And I literally thought it would provide nothing more than beer money. A year later, I'm getting about 3-5 requests a day, it pays my mortgage, and am currently contemplating hiring additional "Assholes" to work for me to keep up with the load.

The point is that Asshole Consulting is scalable, not requiring I immediately quit my daytime job, UNTIL the point in time comes that it is so profitable it compels me to. And even then, because of the nature of the business, I can keep up as it grows by hiring additional employees. You also want to find an idea or establish a company with these same traits.

Fewest Working Parts

During WWII the Germans, by far, had the most advanced tanks in the entire war. A German general was quoted as saying that,

"One German Tiger tank was worth about 10 US Sherman tanks."

When asked how they managed to lose tank battles despite this obvious superiority, he said,

"Because the Americans had tanks #11, 12, and 13."

But whereas the Americans overwhelmed German tanks with

numbers, the Russians had another advantage – fewer working parts.

While the German "Tiger" and "Panther" tanks were still supremely superior to Russia's T-34 tank, the problem the German tanks had was that they were over-engineered. They took too long to produce. They were prone to breaking down. They took too long to repair. There were waaaaay too many working parts in this overly-complicated tank compared to its Soviet counterpart. So even though Tigers were killing three, four, five, even eight T-34's to their one, it took less time to build a new T-34 than it took the Germans to merely repair and re-field a Tiger or Panther. This (among other reasons) is why despite having inferior tanks, the Russians still managed to defeat the Germans.

And when it comes to entrepreneurship, businesses are a lot like tanks.

If I had the choice between starting a new car company or a one-person consultancy (where I am that one person), I would choose the one-person consultancy every time. And the reason is simple – the consultancy has less moving parts, and therefore has less that can go wrong with it.

With a car company you have to worry about:

Unions
Labor
OSHA/safety
Lawyers
Materials
Construction
Sales
Distribution
Lawsuits
Electric bills
The computer network
Network security
Parking lots
Meetings
Sexual harassment suits

and a billion other things.

With the one person consultancy, all I have to worry about is:

Me.

And this is a very important lesson, especially if you're starting your first business. The more moving parts you have, the more that can and WILL go wrong with it.

While it may be tempting to start a nightclub, or design your own clothing line, or create a real-estate empire, keep in mind those businesses all have THOUSANDS of moving parts to them. The people, the machinery, the computers, the contractors, everything, they ALL must be working in perfect order for business to operate smoothly and profitably. But if you have a VERY simple business model, with very few moving parts, less will go wrong, and it will operating at an INSANELY more efficient (and profitable) level.

But before you get worried about computer networks, phone lines, elevators, insurance, and other moving parts that will make your business complex, there is one moving part that is more complicated, more unreliable, and more dangerous than all of them combined.

People.

If you gave me my choice of dealing with a person or dealing with a tornado, I'll choose the tornado. Tornadoes, damaging as they are, are not sentient. They're not conscious. They're acts of nature that are neither evil nor good. They just form when weather conditions are right and lay waste to whatever is in their path. But for all the damage they do, at least they're predictable. You know when they're coming, you know when they're forming, and you know what to do when they're around. Ergo, you can deal with them effectively, no matter how horrible they may be.

Humans have all these drawbacks, minus the predictability.

Humans are selfish, greedy, lazy, and untrustworthy. They can lay waste to your company through lawsuits, devastate your career through a false rape claim, or destroy your family through divorce. But unlike a tornado they are not predictable. Worse still, you will HAVE TO interact with humans in order to run a successful business, if for any other reason than that you have to sell to humans as they are going to be your only client.

Ergo, minimize your risk, especially when you are first starting out. Never hire employees and never take on partners. Employees not only bring about an insane amount of government paperwork and regulation, but they are notoriously unreliable and can always sue you for whatever reason. Partners are worse because TO THIS DAY I have yet to see a partnership where BOTH partners put forth equal amounts of effort. It ALWAYS ends up being one guy who does all the work, while the other guy just spends the money. See if you can find a business that you can do on your own and without hiring a single employee.

Start It Now

Businesses are a lot like flowers. They do not grow overnight. Which is not necessarily a bad thing. Say you did start a company today by your little lonesome and all of the sudden 2 million orders came in the next day.

Could you handle it?
Do you have the man power and equipment to deliver?
Or would you have to turn down a ton of business?

Thankfully, most businesses grow slowly which means you can not only keep up with its organic growth, but if you start NOW in due time it can grow to become something that does replace your day time job. And the sooner you start, the sooner that day will come.

Of course, it will take time, and sadly, it will take failure. Not every business idea works and matter of fact most successful businessmen today failed at least their first three or four times. But with perseverance and dedication inevitably ONE idea will work. And once you find that idea it is to your benefit to have discovered it as soon as possible so you don't have to wait until your 60 for it to finally pay off. So do not delay if you are committed to the path of becoming an entrepreneur. I know people who started in their early 20's to pursue business ideas and today (in their 30's) they answer to no one, work from home, and unlike the remaining 150,000,000 Americans, they love their jobs.

<u>"Yes, You Are An Entrepreneur"</u>

Finally, realize that you don't have to be the next Mark Zuckerberg or Bill Gates to become a successful entrepreneur. When people hear that word they think "billionaires," "tycoons," or "magnates," when in reality an entrepreneur is a man who answers to no one.

For example, the guy who sweeps my chimney.

Not glamorous.
His name is Tim.
You've never met him.
You probably never will.
And you'll be fine with that.

But he charges me $125 an hour to clean my chimney.

And not only is that a handsome wage, he answers to no one, getting to keep all $125 of it.

The truth is being an entrepreneur is more of an independent contractor or "hired gun" nature than it is being some kind of "Mark Cuban Shark Tank Celebrity." You don't need to own a multi-billion dollar corporation as much as you just have to be your own man. You wake up every day doing whatever it is *you want to do*, and above all else *answering to no one*. You make *your* decisions how *you want* them made. Lead *your business* where *you want it led*. And when the revenues come in (and you paid out all of your expenses), *you get to keep all of it*. Not some paltry $7.50 per hour bullshit that your boss "pemitted you to have."

Ergo, entrepreneurship or starting a business shouldn't seem so intimidating when you consider that tradesmen like:

Doctors
Dentists
Mechanics
Electricians
Painters
Barbers
Computer networkers
Chimney sweepers, and
Computer programmers

Are ALL entrepreneurs.

And artists such as:

Dancers
Musicians
Designers
Podcasters, and
Authors,

Are ALL entrepreneurs.

So do not think in order to be an entrepreneur you need to be sitting in some office, watching over 3,000 employees, stuck in meetings all day, while atop a skyscraper smoking cigars you hate and wearing a suit you loathe. It's doing something you like and getting paid for it, no matter what that may be.

Starting a Company

One you get an idea there are four basic steps you will take to start your company. You'll need to:

1. Write a business plan
2. Form a legal business entity
3. Set up a bank account
4. Develop an accounting system

Business Plan

Understand all the time and effort you put into managing, operating, and running a business that in the end FAILS is ultimately wasted time. I don't care how anxious you are about starting a company, being the boss, or making tons of money, the first thing you need to do is self-check your business idea to see if it's even feasible. And you do that by writing a business plan.

Business plans are USUALLY used when you need to approach a bank or an investor when your asking to borrow money or are looking for investors. However, they also serve as a great gut/reality check for entrepreneurs who think they have a good business idea. Therefore, writing a business plan is a vital first step before you even consider starting a business for it not only might come in handy (should you need to approach a bank and borrow money), but it might show you some gaping flaws you overlooked, thereby saving you time (and money) from pursuing a business idea that is doomed to fail.

There are a limitless number of business plan templates out there that you can use, but in general they follow this general format:

Executive Summary – This is a synopsis of your business plan that is (primarily) used by bankers, investors, and other interested parties in your business. It gives them an abbreviated version of your business plan if they just want to give it a quick overview.

Company Description – This explains the company, in detail, regarding what it's going to do, what it's going to sell, who it plans on selling to, and other pertinent information about your company.

Product/Service – This segment goes into detail about your products/services, what you plan on charging for them, where they are made/manufactured, how they are delivered, and other information relevant to your products.

Market Analysis – Here is where you do a THOROUGH and COMPLETE analysis of your market, your competitors, pricing, margins, and the estimated percentage of the market you expect to capture. It is also where you will derive your total sales figures, of which you will base your estimated financial projections upon.

Management Bios – Investors and lenders are going to want to know who is going to be in charge of the company as well as the key people managing it. The IT guy, your chief financial guy, who is doing the accounting, and who is in charge of operations. Essentially, the resumes of any important person who will be involved in the ownership and management of the company.

Financial Projections – Finally, people (least of all, you!) will want to know if the company stands a chance of being profitable. To do this you will run financial projections, using the various data from your previous research. Estimated pricing, volume, and revenues, as well as estimated costs in terms of labor, insurance, utilities, taxes, etc. I cannot emphasize enough how important it is that you hire a competent financial or accounting guru to help you with this as well as explain it to you. Because if you goof this up you can lose a lot of money, not to mention go bankrupt, lose your house, and a score of other horrible and crippling financial ailments.

Again, there are many and much more detailed templates you can use, but regardless of its complexity it is very well worth your time to put together a business plan for your own sake and success.

Form a Legal Business Entity

Once you've done your homework and are convinced this is a business idea worth pursuing, your next step is to create a legal entity through which you will own and operate your business. The reason for a "separate legal entity" is two-fold.

1. To keep your business' finances separate from your personal finances and
2. To protect yourself legally

Without going into a long and lengthy legal explanation, corporations and companies are considered separate legal entities from the individuals that own them. That's why you can own shares in IBM or Apple and when they get sued you are NOT personally liable for their costs. This concept is no different, except on a much smaller scale. You will own your company, but your company is a separate legal entity. Ergo, if some sue-happy asshole tries to sue you for some work you did, they can't. They have to sue the company you did the work under. And if you keep no cash, no assets, and no nothing in that company, they can't get any of your hard-earned money.

As for keeping your personal finances separate from your company's finances, this is merely good business practice. You need to know for a fact that your company is profitable. You can't be putting more cash in, confusing or combining personal with business expenses, or sharing the same bank accounts, never distinguishing what is your company's money and what is your personal money. It is also a VERY GOOD thing to do to prevent getting in trouble with the IRS. People are often tempted to mix business with personal in an attempt to evade taxes. The IRS is not unaware of this. Matter of fact, it's acutely aware of this. Ensure to keep separate and accurate financial records for yourself and for your company.

Knowing the importance of separating your legal and financial "lives" from yourself and your company, you then need to decide which kind of legal business structure you're going to choose. There are pro's and con's to the various types of business structures available to you, but they basically boil down to four primary legal forms:

Sole Proprietor – Technically, this is not a separate legal entity, but people still use it because they're too lazy. They don't bother setting up a corporate entity, merely operate under their own name, and then (if they do) keep separate financial records and accounts for their "company" and themselves. Since this is not a separate legal entity you are not going to want to just be a "sole proprietor." You'll want to set up something with legal protection.

LLC - An LLC or "Limited Liability Company" is the preferred choice of smaller entrepreneurs. Depending on the state you set it up in, it can have as few as one owner or 20. Because you are registering this company with your state, there is a fee that you will have to pay. However, this fee is typically small and it grants you a separate legal entity from which to own and operate your company.

S Corps – An S Corp or "S Corporation" is a legal entity deigned to be for slightly larger companies that are so large they require a board of directors, an executive management team and other more formal managerial arrangements. It is NOT considered a "public corporation" or "C-Corp" which are the large, multi-billion dollar corporations we are all familiar with (Disney, IBM, Nike, etc.) However, the benefit of an S Corp is that it is not taxed. While C Corps such as Wells Fargo, Ford, and Samsung are taxed as corporations, S Corps do not pay taxes. However, do not get excited. While S Corps are not taxed, the money paid out to the individual owner is. So (just like an LLC) your company will not pay a tax on its profits, but you will.

C Corps – Finally, there is the "C-Corps" or as mentioned before your "normal" well-known corporations. These are so large and atypical that most entrepreneurs (unless starting a multi-billion dollar company) are not going to have any use or purpose for them.

There are many other legal entities you can choose from, but for all practical points and purposes, just form an LLC. It's very easy, provides everything a budding entrepreneur needs, and at anytime you can simply change legal entities should your company grow or change that it becomes necessary. To form one, all one has to do is go to your state government's "Secretary of State's" website and they should have a page that allows you to register or "form" a company. You fill out some forms, provide the state with some information, and within a couple days you should have your very own "company." I would only advise considering the state you register your LLC in as some states are tax free (Wyoming, South Dakota, Texas, Nevada, etc.) and other states absolutely hate businesses and tax them to death (New York, California, Massachusetts, Illinois, etc.).

Bank Account/s

Once you establish a legal business entity you will take your paper (that the Secretary of State will mail to you) that certifies you own a company to a bank of your choosing. There you will set up whatever bank accounts you need to operate your firm. Checking, savings, perhaps a line of credit (consult your banker to see what they recommend). Once you fund those accounts with your own personal money you should be ready to go and start operating your business.

However, you may also want to consider opening up a corporate credit card. This may take a while as your business needs to build up its credit, however it is a HUGE time saver in several regards. One, it allows you to make corporate purchases anywhere, not having to make them on your personal credit card and then reconciling them later for accounting purposes. And, two, most credit cards consolidate and categorize expenses making things a lot easier for your accountant when it comes to tax time.

Accounting System

With a legal entity and funded bank accounts you are finally ready to start your first day of operations. However, before you even cut your first check, you absolutely need to have an accounting system in place.

If I were to estimate it, the lack of a good, reliable accounting system accounted for about 80% of the bankruptcies and defaults I witness in my banking career. And if you are a fan of any of the "restaurant" or "bar" turn around shows, 100% of the time the owners have absolutely NO accounting controls whatsoever. But what's truly sad is that if just some simple, basic accounting methods were in place not only would many of these people NOT have filed for bankruptcy, they would have known what the problems were in their companies, allowing them to fix them, resulting in highly profitable companies. Instead, they found accounting "boring," or it "wasn't their thing," which only led them to complete and total financial ruin.

Do not let that be you.

Accounting does not have to be complicated and, ultimately, it can be outsourced. But however you do it, it HAS TO BE DONE. To that end I recommend you do the following:

1. Take a course in basic accounting. It can be online, a free tutorial, or a ton of You Tube videos, but you NEED to understand accounting and financial statements.

2. Hire an accountant. You don't need an accountant full-time, but you do need an accountant from time to time to confirm (on a quarterly basis) you are doing your accounting correctly. Keep him/her around until you are comfortable you are doing it right.

3. Learn Quickbooks. There are many accounting methods out there (I personally just save all my receipts in a shoe box and then compile them at the end of the year), but Quickbooks is a great way for a beginner to get their toes wet AND makes things a lot easier than drafting your own accounting system from scratch.

4. Failing that try my shoe box approach. Save all your business related receipts in a box as well as credit card and bank statements. If savvy enough, compile an income statement and then give it to your accountant. If you're not too sure of your spreadsheet and income statement compilation skills, just drop it off with your accountant and have them work their magic.

If you take the time to do all these things (draft a business plan, keep your business accounts separate from personal, register an LLC, and implement a good accounting system) you will increase your chances of running a successful business multi-fold.

Prepare to Work

I received a business proposal from a client. It was without a doubt the worst business plan I ever read. It had egregious grammatical errors, completely wrong words, numbers that didn't add up, and financial statements that made no accounting sense whatsoever. But the worst part of the business plan was the management section.

All it said was:

"We will outsource management."

Since I am an asshole and I run "Asshole Consulting," I did what any asshole would do.

I reamed the hell out of him.

For the truly insulting thing wasn't that he was too lazy to spell correctly or take the time to compile at least "decent" financial statements, it was the fact it was so clear he expected to do absolutely no work whatsoever. He viewed work as beneath him. Work was for other lesser, inferior people. He was just going to "outsource management."

He would also fail. And I told him so.

The truth about entrepreneurship is that you both WILL and WILL NOT work harder than the average employee. You WILL work harder than the average worker because factually you will. You will put in more hours than the average US worker. You will work HARDER and more focused during those hours. And you will likely work weekends unlike your "working stiff" counterparts.

However, while you'll certainly be working more in terms of volume and intensity, you'll be suffering less because the work is enjoyable, challenging, and purposeful. And in this sense you'll be working less. You won't be filing or faxing. You won't be answering to an idiot boss. You won't be sitting in insufferably long meetings. You'll be leading, managing, creating, and innovating. Of course, there will be times you have to file, fax, or other menial labor (to this day I still have to do data entry), but it will be for YOUR company, 100% benefiting you. It is this that will give you (and all other entrepreneurs) the energy and drive to become successful.

Still, at the end of the day it is all work. You can expect to spend at least 60 hours a week just to make your business successful, and even more if your company starts to take off. Matter of fact, a sad irony many entrepreneurs face is when their businesses become successful it requires even more of their time as they must "strike when the iron is hot." Sadly, it becomes so consuming it comes at the expense of their families and loved ones, often times ending in divorce. But this is the point about entrepreneurship – it's not so much the money as much as it is the time.

Just as money management is key to escaping poverty, time management is key to establishing a successful business. The reason is very simple, unless you have rich parents you need to BOTH support yourself financially (presumably through a "normal job") while also pursuing your entrepreneurial adventure. And, unfortunately, you got the same measly 24 hours all the rich kids have whose parents will front them the money to start their own business.

This leaves you with two options when it comes to pursuing your entrepreneurial endeavor.

One, "The Two Pronged Approach."
Two, "Security is Security."

The "Two Pronged Approach" I also call "Embrace the Suck" because that's precisely what you're going to be doing. You are going to embrace the suckiness of life that is about to come your way. The reason is simple – you are essentially going to be working two jobs. Your daytime job to keep you alive and housed, and your business venture that will (hopefully) make you rich or at least independent. My original "Embrace the Suck" period was where I attended school full time while working full time (so I didn't have to take student loans). When I realized I hated banking and needed to get out, this was followed by another "Embrace the Suck" period where I was a banker during the daytime, a ballroom dance instructor at night, and a developer of online finance classes late at night. But, like all successful business men, my first two business ideas failed, and so I needed to "enjoy" yet another period of "Embracing the Suck." This time I would work the night shift as a security guard while writing books. This one finally paid off.

However, for all the success I may have today, the road to get here was insanely painful. During college I could afford tuition, but barely. I dropped from 150 pounds to 118 my freshman year due to malnutrition and sleep deprivation. During my banking days I was also sleep deprived, but the stress of the work volume drove me into a deep depression and an unhealthy reliance on alcohol to manage my sleep schedule. And my final run at embracing the suck resulted in a deficit of vitamin D (from never seeing the sun) and unrecoverable damage to my social life (because people were asleep when I was awake).

In short, there's no way to sugar coat it – your life is going to equally suck should you pursue the two pronged approach. There's no way around it. There just isn't enough time in the day. Mentally, physically, socially, sexually, sleep-wise, you WILL suffer. It's the price you are going to have to pay.

However, there is a tweak to this two-pronged approach that makes it a lot easier. And it involves the job I've always held (at least in a part time capacity) since I was 18. Security.

"Security is Security" is a much smarter approach than the raw "Two Pronged Approach." It technically is the two pronged approach, but instead of working one job for survival and your other job pursuing your business venture, you combine them into one. And working security allowed me to do just that.

While attending college, I was able to get the occasional security shift that allowed me to not only make money, but work on my homework as well. While writing "Bachelor Pad Economics," the only reason I could write the 512 page book in three months was because I was cooped up in an office for 16 hours a day with nothing to do. If there was one variable that made my achievements and accomplishments possible in life, it was security.

Now this doesn't mean that we should all go join a security company and work as security guards (but it isn't a bad idea). Usually, you have to "earn" yourself the right to work a "desk job" which means outdoor patrols, working overnights, dangerous assignments (bouncing, downtown parking ramps, etc.), lack of sleep, etc. But it does mean we should find some job that allows you to work while on the job. This can be a librarian, a gas station attendant, a "dorm guard," etc. The pay isn't great, but it doesn't have to be. It just has to be "enough" to put food on the table, but allow us to work on our business ideas.

But keep in mind, no matter how beneficial this effective "double dipping" is to your life and your business, there is going to be a price to be paid. The pay is low. Your social life will suffer. And sadly the best time to work on your business during these security-like-jobs is overnight (because you are not constantly interrupted by people).

Don't Be a Fucking Moron

I had a roommate who was an alcoholic, drug addict, thief, and pothead. He was in such bad financial shape he resorted to blowing guys in town to make rent (and support his drug habits). However, the rent was on time, he never brought his problems home, and we actually became pretty good friends. Because of this we went out frequently and over drinks he would let me in on his "latest plan" to escape poverty and make it big. None of them stood a shot in hell, but one that was particularly delusional was when one day he just decided he would declare himself a "business manager."

What was he managing?

His buddy who played guitar.

And how would they make money?

Well, he'd pitch his buddy's guitar playing to various music establishments in town.

I didn't take him seriously until we were about to go out for drinks again and he donned a suit jacket and dress shoes.

I looked at him and said, *"Why are you wearing that? You never wear that!"*

He responded, *"Well, I'm a business manager now. I have to take my job seriously."*

Last I heard he was doing some prison time out west.

The moral of the story is a simple one when it comes to starting and running a business – don't be a douche.

Specifically, don't let the fact you're an entrepreneur get to your head, leading you to make stupid decisions.

My all time favorite is when somebody merely registers an LLC at the Secretary of State's office, and then goes out and makes business cards that say, "President" on it.

President of fucking what? President of fucking nothing.

It's not until you actually make it big and make millions that you should be flashing your card around claiming you're "President" of some company.

Or (one the ladies are particularly guilty of) renting an office, calling it your "global headquarters," and then decorating it with the most expensive and unnecessary stuff just because "they want to have an office." I call this "Playing Make Believe Business" because you aren't doing it because it's a wise decision. You're doing it because you think it's "fun" or "cute" and want to have your own office. This is one of the largest and biggest mistakes a beginning entrepreneur can make. You do NOT want an office. Offices cost money. My office is my bed until I get my lazy ass out of it and move upstairs to my other office, "the couch." Sometimes, if I need to I go to my branch office, "the bar."

That is how business is done in the internet age.

Finally, bragging.

Whatever you do, do not brag about starting a business. Whether you're successful or not it just attracts the wrong type of people. Gold-digging women, people who want to hit you up for money, sue-happy people, stiff-arm-robbing thugs, mafioso type guys that might shake you down. Every element of societal scum that looks to live off of other people are always look for a fat wallet. Do not advertise the fact you might have one (whether you really do or not).

Black Owned Businesses

A final bit of advice is to take full advantage of state, federal, and sometimes local governments' programs that give a certain percentage of their contracts to minority owned businesses. It is a form of affirmative action and you once again may have moral qualms about it, but don't think it is only minorities that are taking advantage of this. I ran into many companies that were effectively owned by white men, but used their wives or minority friends as "puppet heads" of their companies to get government contracts. So, again, do yourself the simplest of courtesies and at least look into it.

To learn more visit the Minority Business Development Agency http://www.mbda.gov

CHAPTER 8
WOMEN

The topic of women is one that cannot be summarized in one little chapter, let alone a billion books. However, since this book is about escaping poverty, accumulating wealth, and is generally financial in nature, we will be addressing the topic of women in that context. Therefore, if you want to learn

"How to meet girls"
"How to nail girls"
"How to impress girls"
etc.,

you'll have to go somewhere else (though a 58 page chapter is dedicated to this topic in "Bachelor Pad Economics" and I would STRONGLY recommend reading it). But if you want to successfully navigate your financial life, especially as it pertains to women, this is a vital and necessary chapter.

The Female Paradox

To be blunt, women are dangerous. And the reason they're dangerous is they are a man's largest paradox. They are both the greatest potential source of happiness, as well as the greatest potential source for misery and pain.

If you find the right woman she can make all the difference in the world. She will support you, be your best friend, satisfy every imaginable sexual desire and need you have, raise your children, and be the single greatest thing in your life. But if you find the wrong one she can fight you, drain you, ruin you, make your life miserable, destroy your children, emotionally destroy you, bankrupt you, and become the bane of your existence. Sadly, for most men, having women in your life is not optional. You are genetically programmed to pursue them, putting them at the top of your priority list. You are designed and engineered to live your life around them, spending the majority of your finite time and life pursuing them. Alas, this is why they are so dangerous. The potential rewards are so great, you cannot help but try to incorporate them into your life in some capacity or another, which gives them the position of power to utterly and totally destroy you.

Because of this women need to be approached in just as serious a manner as your education, your career, your life, and your health. You cannot be naïve or ignorant about their nature and the danger they represent. Because the worst thing that could happen to you is you play all your cards right, clawing and battling your way out of poverty, sacrificing and suffering today for a better tomorrow, finally making a great and better life for yourself, only to have it all stolen and destroyed by a woman because you were thinking with the wrong head.

So take heed because the woman/women you choose to have in your life can make you or break you.

An Alternative - Avoid Women

A very simple solution to dealing with the quandary women present is to simply avoid them. To not have them in your life.

This is a bit of an extreme measure, but some men do prefer to be perpetual bachelors, never having women play any significant role in their love or social lives. To what degree they eschew women, however, depends. Some men are particularly extreme preferring to have NOTHING to do with women. These men are like Nikola Tesla, focusing 100% of their efforts on their own lives and endeavors, and go on to achieve great individualistic things. Other men are merely "perpetual bachelors" who absolutely enjoy the company of a woman, but do not prioritize them in their lives. Men like Benjamin Franklin, President James Buchanan, and Hugh Hefner. And then there are some men who enjoy the company of women, want them in their lives, perhaps even want to marry, but are afraid of the legal and governmental ramifications of marriage. Many of these men come from divorced or fatherless families and simply do not want to repeat the mistakes of their fathers.

However, whatever level of "avoidance" these men decide to choose, consciously or unconsciously, they are rejecting what is no doubt the greatest potential single source of happiness in their lives.

In rejecting women (either through simple misogyny or legitimate fear and concern) they cut out what can and historically has been a man's greatest reason to live.

So before you go this route consider something.

Every man of every race has within them this dream or euphoria. It is the dream of meeting this wonderful woman who you are madly in love with who will make you happy in your life. You may have never met this woman, you may have never even ran into one that could invoke such feelings, but the reason those feelings exist is because in the past your forefathers were lucky enough to meet, fall in love with, and live with such wonderful women. So powerful and strong was their love and relationship with these women, it was embedded in their DNA, and consequently passed on down to you. Sadly, however, not all of your forefathers were lucky enough to experience this powerful and unimaginable love. Most, frankly, endured marginal marriages, sometimes poor ones. However, it was those lucky few that were fortunate enough to find that true love of their life. And so strong were their relationships that those minority of instances overrode the majority of others, instilling within you the knowledge and concept of what such a love would be. And deep down inside you know what that feeling is and what that kind of life would be like.

Statistically speaking, it is unlikely you or I will ever fall in love that strongly. It just really is that rare. But if you purposely cut women out of your life, you guarantee you will NEVER be able to enjoy that happiness and bliss. Matter of fact, in choosing to kick women out of your life, you destroy one of the few things that really makes life worth living for, and it is a route (no matter how badly women may have treated you) I do not recommend.

Ergo, while choosing to live a life without women is very easy and risk free, I do not recommend it. Every man deserves their shot at that rare and uncommon love. Even if the chances are like winning the lottery.

Don't Fuck Up

Since it's likely you're going to prefer to have women in your life, you're going to have to be able to ignore your biological programming, ignore your sexual desires, and approach women in a logical, emotionally-free manner. For as I said before, the key to success is not to fuck up. And if there is a reason men have fucked up, it's because they thought with their dick or their heart, and not their brain.

No matter what your heart or groin tells you, women today are NOT what they were back in the 1950's. While you and I and every other red-blooded male wants and desires a June Ward or Leona Horne type woman in our lives, the truth is women have changed and changed for the worse.

There are many reasons for this. Feminism, misandry, politics, and the government replacing men, but regardless of the reason, women today do NOT put men first in their lives. They do NOT put a husband at the top of their priority list. They do NOT wish to find a man that they can love and cherish for the rest of their lives. They place more value on their careers, their educations, their friends, their illegitimate children, and their traveling. Men come damn well near dead last when it comes to a modern day woman's priority list.

However, while women may have rejected men (and family) as their primary point and purpose in life, they still have not fully accepted the consequences and responsibilities of that decision. Specifically, they still require men to support them. This is not debatable or even questionable as it is evident in a whole host of examples and instances throughout society where women still require the financial and material resources of men to survive.

The "heroic" single mother who constantly collects a government check which is disproportionately paid for by men.

Her same kids that attend the public schools, once again, disproportionately paid for by childless men.

Their education in all of the bullshit degrees of "communications,"

"English," and whatever other nonsensical poppycock they major in. Again, MEN paying the taxes to subsidize their tuition.

An entire industry of make work government jobs as "social workers," "teachers," "non-profit directors," etc. All staffed by women, but paid for from the tax dollars of men.

Health care where women and their children consume thrice the amount of medical services men do. Paid for by men.

And let us not forget that women live longer, allowing them to collect more in social security and medicare, once again disproportionately afforded to them by men.

This insane level of charity and subsidy (no matter how well-intentioned) has resulted in a culture and mentality of entitlement. And this mentality has ruined most women for most men. Most women now think they "deserve" and are "entitled" to a great and many things. Housing, health care, education, child care - things that were the preserve of men just a few short decades ago, but has since been replaced by the government. Unfortunately, this means you, me, and every other man is now faced with a dating pool of (nothing short of) delusional, entitled females who are incapable of selflessness, altruism, and true love. Worse, many of them have become feral and amoral, viewing men as nothing more than tools by which to get resources. Because of this, the modern day man has to be guarded and vigilant about protecting what he worked so hard for from these feral and malicious women.

Sadly, both your hormones and women's ability to be deceitful will plot against you. You'll see a girl you like and your brain will automatically shut off. However, there are some basic principles and rules you can follow that will not only protect you from the malicious females out there, but also help you screen for the good ones that might be marriage material.

#1 Don't Get a Girl Pregnant

Desmond Hatchett, if you don't know him, is quite the charismatic and charming dude. So charismatic and charming he managed to have 30 children by the age of 33. Of course, he's dumber than shit because the fucktard didn't know to wrap up his dick while fucking all those women. So now Desmond doesn't have a life anymore. He can't afford to support 30 dependents, let alone himself, and no matter how good he plays his life game going forward, it's ruined because of the sheer volume of other humans he's brought into this world.

THE

SINGLE

WORST

THING

you can do in your life is have a kid you can't afford.

Doesn't matter if the government is paying for it or the woman lives in another state. They will come after you for child support and it is an albatross that will be hanging around your neck until you die. The Civil War might as well have not been fought for you, because that's essentially what your life will be if you have an illegitimate kid – a slave to the government.

#2 Don't Stick Your Dick in Crazy

One in four American women are on some kind of mental health drug. And that does not account for the fact the younger they are the higher percentage are on some kind of drug. So when you're dating realize there's a TON of batshit insane women out there.

But what makes it worse is women are MASTERS at faking sanity.

I've dated women where their true psychotic nature did not materialize or present itself until I was a full three months into dating them. This, unfortunately, is about the time you start to develop feelings for them and makes it really hard to accept this reality. Still, reality is reality, and there are a ton of batshit insane women.

The trick is to identify these women early on so you not only avoid them, but never get into the position of actually falling for them in the first place. And while there are no "black and white" specific guidelines to identifying batshit insanity, there are some red flags that give it away.

Drama, crying, bulimia, crime, victimhood, poor finances, "I'm bi-polar," lithium in the medicine cabinet, other men's children, hypocrisy, and all other sorts and manners of psychotic behaviors. There is no complete compendium on the "list of traits psychotic women have" but you should be able to know it when you see it. And when you see it, run the other way. Life is too short and too precious to be dating crazy, let alone impregnating it.

#3 Don't Stick Your Dick in Ebola

The cold, harsh, mean, reality-based fact is that the black community has the highest rates of STD infections. You can get upset about that fact or you can accept it and start protecting yourself. I suggest you protect yourself.

This doesn't mean you don't date a sister you are absolutely enamored with. But it does mean you wrap your fucking shit up or require an STD test before you start dating a girl seriously. The reason is not because of distrust or even your own sexual health (which are good enough reasons on their own), but because if you ever want to find, date, or marry a quality girl, if you got "Ebola Dick" your chances are over. It is not for you or the local sweaty whore you're about to bang, it's for that quality girl you may want to settle down with someday. So do yourself and that future goddess a favor and ensure you don't get "Ebola Dick."

#4 Avoid False Rape Claims

A sad consequence to the inordinate amount of money, attention, and resources that have been plowed into American women is that they are not only entitled, but have become ego maniacs. And some (not all) are so egotistical they have no problems making up fake rape accusations.

This is an unfortunate topic I wish didn't have to be discussed, but the consequences of being accused of rape are so severe it has to be addressed. There IS a certain statistical percentage of women who will resort to lying about being raped to either get revenge on you (for dumping her, not calling her back, etc.) or beget attention from the community. This phenomenon is especially pronounced on college campuses where a fanaticism about "rape culture" has ensued, resulting in nothing short of a witch hunt for men who were accused of "rape." Sadly, "rape" is now being redefined to include "unwanted advances," drunken sex, or mere "regret" when a woman regrets sleeping with you the next day.

This, again, falls under the "don't stick your dick in crazy" category and it is hard to determine what woman will falsely accuse you of rape. However, instead of trying to predetermine traits and qualities that would suggest a girl will falsely accuse you of rape, it is recommended you get hard evidence that your sexual encounters were mutual and agreed upon. The "after sex happy text" is one of the simpler methods. Merely text a girl after a night of fucking saying, "Hey, that was great, thanks for last night." Usually she will respond in kind with an equally positive text. SAVE THAT TEXT as proof you did not indeed "rape her." There are other methods (have a camcorder in your bedroom, don't date feminists, don't have booze around, etc., etc.,) but the point is society has degraded this far that these measures are unfortunately necessary. You simply cannot afford being accused of rape, no matter how false that accusation may be.

#5 You're Not the Daddy

In addition to false rape claims, women have deteriorated enough in America that some will falsely accuse you of "being the daddy" of their child. And not only will they falsely accuse you, but many will ensure you ARE the daddy by impregnating themselves with your sperm they found in a condom or their mouths.

Tom Leykis (a radio show host EVERYONE OF YOU MUST LISTEN TO) put it best.

Each sperm cell of yours is like a little credit card. And the women know this.

If they can get your sperm and get impregnated (even if you were using protection) they will. And not only to satisfy their "Darwinistic desires" of having children, but to trap you into supporting them. This particularly disgusting and dishonest scam I found at first to be unbelievable. But all it takes is a simple search on the internet of "how to trick my boyfriend into getting me pregnant" and you will be shocked as to just how many MILLIONS of women have no moral qualms about tricking you into getting them pregnant.

This is a REAL threat and, like false rape accusations, is so severe you need to take measures to ensure it doesn't happen to you. To that aim you ALWAYS flush your condoms down the toilet, ensure she swallows, take male birth control, or consider getting a vasectomy. Your life and yourself are too damn precious to have it ruined by a woman who steals your sperm and then forces you to be a father when you never wanted to be. Ensure it doesn't happen.

#6 Avoid Bad People

We alluded to this before in a previous chapter, but if you hang around bad people, bad things tend to happen to you, no matter how good you might be.

And with women, it's the same thing.

You can hang out with the girls, snapping their fingers, bragging about being "baby mama's" spreading their legs for any guy who comes their way. You can go to the night clubs where all the popular girls are, who simply wait a little bit longer before they spread their legs for a slightly stronger, bigger man. But in the end, you're fishing in a toxic environment and any "fish" you catch aren't going to be worth it.

This isn't to say you have to go to church to find a "nice girl," (which isn't a bad idea) but you do have to have the self respect to chose a woman for yourself that is of quality and caliber. So consider places like school, like the church, like the community center, ballroom dance club, etc., where you might find a traditional girl that is looking for a higher-quality guy such as yourself.

#7 Keep Your Currency Up

Much as it may sound like you're the one doing the "shopping" for a wonderful girl, you also have to realize it ain't a one way street. You too must bring something of value or worth to the table, otherwise what quality girl is going to go out with you? Unfortunately, this means you have to commit the time and resources to become a quality, upstanding man. Lifting weights, dieting, staying in shape are all requirements, but you also must be accomplished, driven, charismatic, charming, funny, witty, and all other manners of adjectives that make girls want and desire you.

This, like a good scotch, takes time. It's why an old fart like me can run circles around a physically superior 24 year old kid when it comes to picking up girls. Because I am old and wise enough to know to smile with an eye-brow-raised-Denzel-Washington look at them, posing in a certain manner, telling them PRECISELY what they want to hear, tickling their fancies, and making them want to go out on the dance floor with me. However, this is decades of experience and there is no other way to gain it other than living it.

In the meantime, though, before you become the (ahem, cough, cough, wheeze, wheeze) "refined Cary Grantish gentleman" I am, you simply need to avoid fucking up. The charm and charisma will develop as you age, but if you simply play your cards right you will be AMAZED how much of a valuable commodity you become. If you simply:

1. Don't have kids
2. Don't get divorced
3. Don't have an STD
4. Stay in shape
5. Don't file for bankruptcy
6. Don't do drugs

you WILL BE in the top 5% of men by the age of 30 and will be one of the most sought after commodities by women.

Not because of anything you did, but merely because of what you DIDN'T DO.

So as long as you avoid bad girls and bad situations, while keeping your own nose clean you will be in a supremely better position than most to find a quality love of your life and consequently live a supremely better life.

Finding the Right Girl

Once you've managed to avoid the bad girls, it's time to go on the hunt for a good girl. And while no man has perfected the art of identifying and winning the heart of a "good girl," we definitely have made some mistakes you can learn from which will go a long way in saving you the time and heart ache your elders have suffered. However, the key thing is to realize the importance of finding and selecting the right girl. Remember, the difference between a full life, replete with happiness and mirth and that of a miserable life where one contemplates suicide daily is simply choosing the wrong woman. Thus, it's of vital importance to your life that you vet these women thoroughly.

Where Is Her Daddy?

The majority of problems the US faces today can be traced to the lack of a father in the household. Whether it be alcoholism, crime, or shorter life expectancies, children without a father present are children that suffer and under-perform. Sadly, it may not be a girl's fault her dad was a deadbeat or her mother divorced, but in the end women who do not have good and strong relationships with their father's are damaged goods.

I cannot emphasize enough the importance that the girl you intend to date or marry knows and loves her father. You actually WANT to walk up to the house, see the old man with the shotgun pointing at your face because that indicates the girl has been exposed and educated about men and knows to love and cherish them. If the father is gone, absent, or was never around in the first place, sadly, you're likely going to have to run. Because that girl's upbringing has been skewed by her mother which more often than not leads to mental problems, hatred and distrust for men, and a government-check-induced entitlement mentality.

This isn't to say you can't find a fatherless girl that is sane and would make a decent life partner. But it is to say it's very difficult and the largest factor to consider when looking for a good girl.

<u>No Baby Mama's</u>

Do yourself the least bit of courtesies and self-respect. Do not date, wed, or marry single moms. Yes, there's always the caveats and exceptions, but the reality still remains that when you date a single mother you are

1. In third place behind her and her child (fourth if "Jesus" is involved)
2. Not the guy she really wanted as she fucked some other dude
3. Raising another man's children

None of which is acceptable to a self-respecting man.

I don't care how much the media, politicians, and Hollywood promote, propagandize and worship "single moms," in the end they're women that made bad choices, brought innocent children into this world without the reliability and stability of a suitable father. And be it through the state or the men they date, they now require other men to support their mistakes.

You deserve a woman who is not the mother of another man's child. You have the right to your own family and your own children. And if women are too enamored with sleeping with the bad boys, spitting out children they truly don't care for, all so they can collect a government check, those are women your life is just too short and valuable to be wasted upon.

<u>She Supports Herself</u>

Thanks to feminism, long gone are the days where the man was the bread winner and supported the household. Now women are "equal" and need to be treated as such. However, the majority of them merely want the benefits of being equal without any of the responsibilities. This has resulted in, frankly, a hypocrisy that is perpetrated upon men every day.

Women are "equal," but still expect men to ask them out.
Women are "equal," but still expect men to pay for dates.
Women are "equal," but need government money and programs to pay for their education and children.
Women are "equal," but need constant affirmative action to get them jobs.

In the end, what you realize is that women are only equal in their demands for equality, but never for the required work that it takes to be on par with men. Alas, an entire generation of women "claim" to be independent, but still demand men do most of the heavy lifting in society.

Do not settle for one of these hypocrites.

There are a good many REAL women who not only claim to be equals and independent, but carry their weight and support themselves as well, talking the talk and walking the walk. They are rare, but they do exist. And these are the real women you want by your side. Women who know what it takes to support oneself and appreciate a man who supports himself. Women who are skilled and educated in fields that pay well, but without any of the whiny feminist political lip. Women who have no problem carrying their own weight, but also enjoy being women and love independent, strong men.

The irony is that the women who brag the most about being independent are usually the most dependent people on the face of the planet. Single moms, women's studies professors, politicians, etc. And the ones who are most independent usually aren't reminding you every two seconds just how independent they are. Find one of those quiet, genuinely independent ones and keep her.

No Student Debt

In many regards women are liabilities to a man, but nowhere is this more literal than when it comes to student loans.

The truth is most women major in stupid shit. And not only do they major in stupid shit, they take on hundreds of thousands of dollars in debt to get their worthless degrees. Alas, upon graduating with their "Masters in Transgendered Hispanic 14th Century Poetry Studies," not only are they armed with an attitude (because they have a "masters degree") they also have a ton of debt. Debt that will never be repaid with the work they're qualified for (barista). Thus, every year millions of women with trillions in student loans go looking for men to bail them out of their student loan debts.

Do not be one of those men.

You want a woman that is not only truly independent, but financially savvy as well. And this means she's smart enough not to major in stupid crap, let alone go $80,000 in debt for it. Sadly, the vast majority of women do not fit this profile, presenting potential suitors with a financial liability that is not their problem. Ergo, it's vital that you not only find out if a girl you're interested in has student loans, but insist that she is the one to pay for her mistake. If not, you're effectively no different than being the taxpayer bailing out the banker scum in 2008.

No Liberal Arts Majors

Akin to student debts, you want to avoid women who majored in the liberal arts. And the reasons are multiple.

First, most liberal arts majoring women have no valuable or employable skills. Their degrees are largely useless hobbies that they thought would be "fun," resulting only in debt and low employment prospects. You will be carrying them financially if you ever dare to marry a liberal arts major.

Second, most liberal arts degrees are nothing more than programs in leftist political indoctrination. Not to get political, but most women who major in the liberal arts are going to be leftists/socialists/feminists/Democrats. Which there is nothing wrong with per se, bar the fact they will ALWAYS put the government and the state ahead of men. They will always put their "careers" ahead of men. And some of them just outright hate men and blame them for everything. It's not that they can't be deprogrammed, but why would you bother tolerating such damaged goods in the first place anyway? You want an IT girl, an accountant, or a nurse. A woman who lives in the real world and is capable of supporting herself.

Third, arrogance. Liberal arts majors think they're smart simply because they went to college. I've literally heard a woman brag about how she was "smarter" than a chemical engineer because he "only" had a bachelors degree and she had a masters. Women are a pain in the ass enough. You don't need the added attitude and lip that's going to come from a ego-maniacal girl with her "masters" in an easy and worthless field.

No Feminists

No matter what they say, "feminism" is not about the equal treatment of men and women. Feminism is now officially a religion for mentally damaged women. If you don't believe me all you have to do is look up "vaginal knitting" and "menstrual painting." And if that isn't enough for you, just visit your local women's studies department at your local university and see if they aren't batshit insane, hate-filled women.

Sadly, while this may represent some of the more fringe and extreme elements of the religion of feminism, most young women are taken in with the propaganda and actually claim to be feminists themselves. They literally don't know what they're agreeing too, but unfortunately some of feminism's toxic hatred and bigotry against men still manages to seep through. Alas, many women today view normal everyday hurdles as "sexism" or "oppression," which not only turns them into whiny "professional victims," but toxifies them to the point they are not datable and forever purged from being marriage material. Regardless of your politics, do not date feminists.

The Risk of Religious Girls

Religious girls present a slightly more complex problem. Whereas logic would suggest religious girls are of higher quality and caliber, unfortunately many religious girls today are not sincere in their belief, abusing religion for ulterior reasons. These reasons are many and varied, but they usually boil down to being able to live a double standard and control other people.

For example, the notorious "born again Christian girl" did not all of a sudden "find Jesus" in her heart. Most born again Christian girls spectacularly fucked up their life in some regard and instead of accepting responsibility for their actions, found "Jesus" who conveniently "forgives all." They further abdicate responsibility for their failures subscribing to fateism. "The Lord will provide." "God has a plan." This, in an ironic sense, makes many religious girls very arrogant and egocentric because they can do no wrong. Ergo, they don't really believe in "God" or "Jesus dying on the cross," etc., as much as they want an excuse that protects their ego and excuses them from taking any responsibility in their lives.

Another problem you're likely to run into with religious girls is how they will "lord" over you the fact you're not religious (or are simply of a different religion). This puts them in a position of "supremacy" allowing them to bark orders to you, as well as refuse desires you may have of them. This can mean anything from "I can't date you, you don't have Jesus in your heart" to "blow jobs and lingerie are not acceptable in my religion." Again, it has nothing to do with the religion. It has to do with control. Religion is merely the tool they use.

Finally, a common problem many of my religious male friends are running into is their "default rank." If you are religious your god comes first. Ideally, you would put your loved one or spouse at #2, loving them more than yourself at #3. However, most girls' ranks go like this:

#1. God/religion/deity
#2. Themselves
#3. You

So the problem many men face when dating religious girls is they are usually default-ranked #3 making them a pretty low priority in religious girls' lives. Sadly, it gets even worse as most women today carry a little more baggage than merely hypocritically believing in a religion. So you're more likely to see a list like this:

#1. God/religion/deity
#2. Themselves
#3. Their illegitimate children
#4. Mother/family
#5. Their education
#6. Their friends/social life
#7. Their career
#8. Horses (this is more common than you think)
#9. Boyfriend/husband

This isn't to say religious girls are bad or that you can't find one that won't abuse her religion to control you. But it is to warn you the reputation women have for being "good girls" and "marriage material" simply because they're religious is false.

Date Outside Your Race

One of the more shocking things I ran into while doing the research for this book was the number of black men whose mothers (and family in general) viewed dating outside their race as traitorous. Their responses ranged from a mother just shaking her head in shame, dismissing her son as merely being "foolish," to quite violent reactions, accusing their sons of being Uncle Tom's, threatening to kick them out of the house. Whatever the level of disagreement, it's wrong.

Not only is it outdated and outright racist, but it's just plain evil to think you have the right to control who another human being dates. Worse is to threaten your children with disownership should they dare date outside of the race, forcing them to choose between their right to sovereignty over their own lives and their families.

But these moral reasons aside, there is a much simpler reason you should date outside your race – statistics. Blacks again only make up 12% of the US population, leaving you with roughly only 1/8th of the girls to date. You simply increase your chances 800% in being willing to date other races.

Finally, many people are no doubt asking,

*"Why 'The Black **MAN's** Guide Out of Poverty?' What about the women?"*

And I'll be directly blunt and truthful.

I believe black women (as a group) are so spoiled with so much government money and programs, they do not have the desire, nor intellectual honesty to read, let alone adhere to such a book. This isn't to say there aren't independent, quality black girls who would make great girlfriends or wives, but if using the illegitimate birth rate is any sort of proxy, 72% of black women would rather live a life of being wedded to the government than their fellow black man. Additionally, (assuming you have the self-respect to raise your own family, not another man's) the fact these women have other men's children renders the majority of them unmarriageable. This doesn't mean you should not date black women, but the statistics almost force you to date outside your race.

Ultimately, however, it doesn't matter what the color of her skin is. If you find the right girl, that's all that will matter. Just don't pass up on what could be the greatest thing in your life simply because she didn't have the right skin color.

1 in 100

The sad truth is that after you date enough you'll soon realize that a stable, reliable, self-supporting, pro-sex, beautiful, sane girl is incredibly rare. So rare that my own dating experiences put it at 1 in 100. Only ONE girl per ONE HUNDRED is what I would consider marriage material.

This sucks, obviously, because with that low a percentage of women, how are most men supposed to get married and live happy lives?

You're not.

This is why if you find that special girl you should get down on your knees and thank the lord because they really are that rare. Between feminism, society, media, the government, reality TV, and Oprah, most women have been ruined when it comes to being quality, marriage material for men. The challenge is not so much dedicating your time and efforts towards finding such a rare girl, but mentally preparing yourself for the statistical likelihood you're not going to find that "special girl."

To that end, don't try to find a girl that is "perfect." Find a girl that is "good." A girl that will not destroy you, but support you. She doesn't have to be the "end all be all," just a girl who likes you, takes care of you, and supports you. And in today's society, that's rare enough.

None of this Hyphenated Name Bullshit

Finally, one last "red flag" that will be very apparent is a woman who insists on hyphenating her name when she marries. I do not care what the "philosophical" or "political" arguments are, the act of insisting her name be hyphenated shows she is not capable of altruism and selflessness and does not put you first in her life. This is such a clear and obvious sign that while maybe enraging at first, you should be thankful for it because it clearly identifies women who are just not capable of being married. This isn't to say you can't convince a woman to change her name, but if she is adamant, even priding herself that she's going to hyphenate her name when she gets married,

thank her kindly,
turn around, and

run.

Marriage and Cohabitation

After much hunting and searching (and maybe dating a couple girls at the same time), you will either find "the one" or get so sick of the drama and bullshit dating brings that you'll start to want to settle down. However, whereas in the past "settle down" meant marriage, today that is not the case. You have several options when it comes to a committed relationship, many of which may prove a superior arrangement to marriage.

First, marriage is first and foremost for having kids. This is why marriage was a naturally occurring phenomenon across all cultures and religions around the world. Societies realized that to raise successful, self-supporting, contributing children they needed the stability of a mother and a father. Thus, either through the church or the state (or both) men and women took religious and legal vows to stick together. Not so much for themselves, but for the children they would bring into the world AND (ultimately) for the "tribe" as this would ensure illegitimate children would not consume resources, ultimately destroying the tribe.

Regardless, this makes marriage pointless if you aren't going to have kids. And since kids cost a lot of money (not to mention time) many people are opting not to have kids at all. But just because you don't want kids doesn't mean you don't want a spouse or a significant other in your life. So you can either cohabitate or be in a serious relationship with a girl but maintain separate homes.

There are pros and cons to each. Living together you can share expenses, you have the company of one another, and with a combined income you can afford a nicer place. However, some people like their independence and living together will drive them nuts. Thus, having separate dwellings, but still dating is another option.

Regardless of which option you choose, however, keep in mind when you start to get into the world of "marriage" and "living together" the biggest and realest threat of women becomes reality – divorce.

Divorce is the number one ruiner of men's lives. Half of all marriages end in divorce and are initiated by women 70% of the time. Additionally, you don't even have to be married to get divorced. In simply living together for a certain period of time your state government will consider you "married," forcing a government contract and law on you that you never agreed to sign up for. This allows your girlfriend/wife to sue you for half your assets, alimony, and (if you have any kids) child support should she file for divorce.

To avoid all this and mitigate the risk and danger women pose, the first and best thing to do is choose the right girl. The right girl will love you for you, never use you for money, make your life happy, and support you through thick and thin. Unfortunately, it can take years, decades even to find such a quality girl, and even then, women can "fake" being nice for years fooling you into thinking you found "the one." Because of this, even if you do have a quality girl, it is vital you do some "pre-planning" to protect your assets, protect your life, and everything you worked so hard for.

Your Secret Stash

Before you get married or cohabitate it is important you hide a significant percentage of your money either in an account that is not in your name or actual physical cash in a safe or some other hiding place. Because this stash was put away before you met your to-be spouse she will be unaware of it and, should she divorce you, not even to know to go after it.

However, it isn't an issue of just stashing away some cash before you start getting serious with a girl. If you marry, it "should be" till death do you part. This means you'll be building up wealth overtime. Wealth that also needs to be hidden. Here the technique is a bit more methodical where you regularly take out smallish, but significant and random bits of cash. You quietly park these monies in an account of a buddy of yours or perhaps buy silver and gold, squirreling them away somewhere. If done right, you should have at least enough money to "start all over again" if your wife were to divorce you and take "half your assets."

You Are "Poor"

A client of mine faced a problem. He was an INCREDIBLY successful surgeon, but was looking to get married. Most of his life was dedicated towards education and his career, but as he approached the age of 40 he figured he better start working on starting a family. The problem was while he could easily get young, attractive women to go out with him, in the end they would invariably start to expect him to pay for stuff. And not just dates or dinner, but their rent, their car payment, etc. Knowing these were obvious gold-diggers he wanted to figure out how to find girls that weren't.

So I told him to send me pictures of his cars, his house, and his wardrobe. And sure enough, it was precisely what I suspected.

The man was worth millions and it showed. He had a brand new Mercedes, the nicest of clothes, jewelry, an Omega watch, and his house was insane. He was unconsciously advertising the fact he was filthy rich and gold-diggers for miles around could smell it.

My solution was simple.

Get rid of that car and buy a Kia Rio.
Get rid of your house and rent a humble, but nice apartment.
Get rid of your fancy clothes and fancy jewelry and replace it with Wal-Mart clothes.
Oh, and by the way. You're no longer a doctor. You're a nurse or some other lower ranked medical professional. You do NOT let any girl know you're a doctor.

Sure enough, with out all the bling and the flash and the cash, the girls who asked for their "rent to be paid for" or "their student loans to be paid for" went away. I don't know if he was successful in finding a wife just yet, but I do know the money-digging whores are no longer looking to sink their teeth into him.

You have to do the same thing.

Not that you shouldn't own nice things in life, but you do NOT advertise the fact you are rich or successful. You drive a humble car, you do not go on expensive trips, you do not have expensive jewelry or clothes, and if necessary you lie about what you do for a living. This will do two things. One, it will screen out any of the gold-diggers who never had any intention of marrying you, but marrying your money. Two, it will mislead your wife into thinking you "don't have that much money anyway" over the course of your relationship, allowing you to hide your money. Over time, hopefully, you'll find your wife to be trustworthy and then you can "surprise" her by letting her know you were a surgeon this entire time, and that she's an effective millionaire. But in the meantime, you want to make sure your wife loves you for you. And making sure there isn't any money around for her to fall in love with is a smart start.

Pre-nups

A more literal and direct way to protect all you worked for in life is to get a prenuptial contract. This is a legal contract, agreed upon by the man and the woman, that determines how the assets and income will be divided should the marriage (or relationship) end in divorce. The prenuptial contract presents a paradox that if you have to have it signed, then you have the wrong woman. Women will also (somewhat rightfully so) be hurt and offended you dared to suggest or insist on such a thing.

To solve this problem, though, a bit of forthright honesty early on goes a long way. Ensure that any girl you date knows early on that you will not marry unless your future wife signs a prenuptial agreement. Since they are not likely to be emotionally vested in you so early on, they will not take such offense or umbrage to your insistence. However, the fact will be planted in their brains, making it more agreeable should the point in time come you two were to wed.

But while prenuptial contracts seem an effective and simple tool to protect your life's work, they are not 100% effective. They can and have been thrown out by divorce courts. This is in part due to divorce courts being more friendly to women, as well as both the ex (and her lawyer) stand to gain huge sums of money if they can get a prenuptial contract overturned. You will definitely want to have both YOUR LAWYER and HER LAWYER look over the contract before signing it. It may not be romantic, but divorce never is.

CHAPTER 9
FAMILY

The only true source of happiness is other people. And once you find "that special girl" you will have found the single most important human in your life. The question is whether you and the love of your life want to create even more little humans for you to enjoy. Because while (if you did it right) you and your spouse will make each other very happy, children can also be a great source of happiness and love in life.

However, the question of having children is not a light one to make. Matter of fact, it's the single most important financial decision you will ever make in your life because of the sheer cost in terms of both time and money they will require. Additionally, despite how most American parents view their children, children are not "toys" or "things" that you "have" like a luxury SUV or designer shoes. They are fellow human beings with the exact same capacity for pain, misery, suffering, and sentienceness that you have. And if you have them for the wrong reasons or are not capable of rearing them adequately and appropriately, you will be responsible for causing these innocent people immense pain and suffering.

So choose wisely, because it's one thing if you fuck up your life. It's another thing if you fuck up the lives of innocent children.

The Liability of Children

To show you the true costs of children you just have to understand one thing and one thing only about them.

Once you have one your life is over.

It's done.

Your life is now going to be 100% dedicated to them. You brought them into this world, and now you get to take care of them. There's no more going out clubbing every night. There's no more roadtrips at the drop of a hat. There's no more ordering that extra burger. Your time and finances are now going to be put towards the rearing and upbringing of that child. Because if you don't put them ahead of you and your life priorities you are a shitty, pathetic, miserable failure of a parent.

Of course, mere name calling isn't going to threaten a truly ignorant or aloof person into becoming a good parent. Millions of men and women bring children into this world they never had any intention of raising. The child was merely a 10 second orgasm for the man and a cure for baby rabies or perhaps a meal ticket for the woman. Because absolutely no thought was given before bringing these innocent children into the world, the mother and father (if married) are likely to get divorced, or worse, the father was never present in the child's life to begin with.

Alas, the real question you need to ask yourself before you go sticking your unprotected dick into any inviting hole is simply this:

"How fun was it when your parents got divorced?"
"What was it like living in a single parent home?"
"What was it like not having your dad around, or even knowing who your dad was?"
"What was your A.C.E Score (look it up! http://acestudy.org/ace_score) and what kind of A.C.E. score can you expect your children to have?"

Not that every man in America grew up in a broken home, but many of you did. And many of you remember just how painful, stressful, and miserable your childhood was without a stable, two-parent family. That is the EXACT same pain and agony you will wreak upon whatever innocent kids you bring into this world.

So forget the costs of raising a child.
Forget the time it will take to raise a child.

You just think long and hard about whether you want to be responsible for inflicting the same misery and damage you suffered during your childhood on some equally innocent kid.

With that moral lesson out of the way, we also need an economics lesson about children. Children, as mentioned before, are the #1 cause of poverty. The reason why is that they are incredibly expensive. Each kid (depending on whose statistics you want to use) costs roughly $240,000 to raise and that's without college. But worse than the monetary costs are the time costs. Kids, at least until the age of four need CONSTANT supervision. They cannot be left alone at all. This means either you or the mother are going to have the equivalent full-time job of merely watching over your kids. Even if you decide to "outsource" this to daycare, you still need to work up the money to pay for it. But no matter how you "handle it" your time investment costs alone will easily add another $240,000 to the total costs of raising a child.

When all is said and done you will roughly spend half a million dollars in time and money raising just ONE child. And that says nothing about getting sick, losing sleep, losing health, and the lower standard of living you WILL suffer. However, when it's all said and done it will be "all worth it" and you'll "have done it no other way..."

Or at least that's what they say.

For while parents "always" claim their children are the "greatest thing to happen to them" and "they'd do it all over again," this is not always the case.

When surveyed behind closed doors studies show anywhere between 10% to 70% of parents regret having children. While that is quite the range, at least 1 in 10 parents regret having children. Ergo, the issue isn't just whether you spend the required time and money on raising a child, but if you do it right. Because doing it "right" can mean the difference between a happy family life, replete with family gatherings and Christmas dinners, or ostracized kids who don't love you as they let you rot away by yourself in a nursing home.

You don't just owe it to your children to be the best parent in the world. You owe it to yourself as well.

What You Owe to Your Children

If you want to have any shot at a happy and fulfilling family life, you are going to have to invest heavily, intelligently, and consistently into your family. It is also going to require you to be selfless and altruistic, sacrificing yourself for your wife and kids. But in the end, you will not be one of those parents whose children are constantly at the psychologist, blaming everything on you. You will not have your children living in your basement at the age of 33. And you will not be raising your kids' kids because they fucked up in life and got pregnant at 14. You will have a family that loves you and supports you into old age (perhaps even giving you grandchildren). And while there certainly are no guarantees in life, if you provide your children with these six things below, chances are your family will be the greatest experience in your life instead of a miserable nightmare you regret.

#1 A Stable, NUCLEAR Family

The number one variable that will determine whether your children grow up happy, healthy, sane, and productive is if they live in a TWO-PARENT household – aka – a nuclear family. The presence of both a mother and a father provide the children with the discipline, experience, and interaction that is necessary from both sexes, as well as the different forms of love needed to become a functional, mentally healthy adult. The kind, caring, forgiving aspects of a mother, and the tough fatherly love in the form of discipline, logic, reason, toughness, morality, standards, and honor.

Of course, delivering a nuclear family presupposes several things.

One, that there's a *quality mother* present. Did you just stick your dick in crazy and now get to raise a child with an insane woman who is fighting you, screaming at you, and suing you for child support? Or did you find an employed, independent, loving, caring, selfless woman who would put you and the children before her? No family can be successful with some psycho baby mamma running around, thinking she's the center of the universe, demanding things from men and the government while she holds her kids hostage to a life of pure suck. She needs to view you and the children as the most important things in her life. Not tools to get more money, sympathy, or attention.

Two, that there's a *quality father* present. What kind of man are you? Are you also getting your accounting degree? Are you putting in those hours at the office? Are you working hard enough to pay for and support a family? And are you willing to invest the time that is necessary to property raise your children? A mother is only 50% of the equation, and an equally stable, hard-working, and selfless father is also a mandatory for the raising of quality children.

Three, that you truly love your children and commit to spending the time necessary to raise them. If there's something that pisses me off it's where two "high income earning" parents decide they want children, but are too busy with their "oh so important careers" that neither have the time to actually raise them. They simply "outsource" the upbringing of their children like a US company does jobs to China. So instead of mom and dad raising their children, it's the nanny, the daycare facility, or the public schools with their "before and after school programs." The truly sad thing about this is that they never cared about the children in the first place. They merely viewed their children as things to have like a luxury SUV or fancy drapes that go well with the house.

In short, to have a nuclear family, you just can't have married parents, but parents who are also present and actively engaged in the lives of their children. This means everything from spending time at dinner, disciplining them, rewarding them, and above all else, playing with them. No parents are going to become the perfect "Heathcliff Huxtable" type family. But they don't have to be. They just have to be married, present, and there.

#2 Adequate Finances

Since children are so expensive it's a pretty good idea to be able to afford them before you start bringing them into this world. Because if you don't, then a whole host of people are going to suffer.

First, you and the mother are going to suffer because what inadequate money you do have will be wiped out as it is primarily used to pay for your children.

Second, your parents and family members now have to take over baby sitting and child-rearing operations because (it's likely) neither you nor the mother make enough money on your own to support a family. This means both of you have to work and now family members get to raise children that aren't their responsibility. I'm sure that's exactly what your parents wanted to be doing during retirement.

Third, the taxpayer gets to pay more in taxes. Since you can't afford your children and the government is only more than happy to replace you with a check, politicians will vote in programs that force the rest of the country to work that much harder to pay for your mistake. At first this may sound great, "free money." But remember, that government check is usurping your role in society and replacing you. Additionally, keep in mind if you're one of the guys that doesn't "fuck up," it will be your taxes that will be increasing to pay for others' mistakes.

There are other victims, but in the end the true victims are (as always) going to be the children. And not just because you won't be able to afford them nice things (you won't) or that money will be a constant worry (it will), but because of the lack of time you will have to spend with them.

Shipping them off to daycare.
Shipping them off to grandma's.
Shipping them off to pre-school.
Shipping them off to the neighbors.
All so both of you can work to "maybe" afford that child.

They will have no time with their parents. And even if you do make enough money to afford them, it is all moot if you can't spend time being there with them. Thus, it is vital you make enough money so that both you and the mother get to spend enough time with your own children, not merely paying for them.

#3 Actual Parenting

Closely related to #2 is actually parenting your kids. Again, it angers me to no end when I see those rich parents, with all the money in the world, value their career and themselves more than their children, outsourcing their children to daycare or a nanny. It behooves the question,

"If you didn't want to raise them, then why the fuck did you have them????!!!!!"

No amount of daycare providers or nannies is a substitute to a mother. No amount of after-school programs or pre-school programs is a substitute for a father. The reason is that your children want YOU as their parents, not some unrelated strangers whose faces change every year.

Because of this the OPTIMAL form of parenting is one person stays home, while the other one works. This is not an opinion, this is not a preference, it's how human kind has evolved over the years and is the most efficient and beneficial family structure for raising children. Unfortunately, because of the poor economy (and how younger people are disproportionately disaffected by it), it is not always possible for a family to get by on one income.

Tough.

Suck it up.

There are countries where families live on a fraction of what we do here in the US and they still manage to have either a mother or father stay home to rear the children. Additionally, during the "ideal" 1950's the June and Ward Cleaver nuclear families of the world managed the same with incomes of 1/3 today's. What you have to do is some incredible and crafty budgeting (as well as suffering), but it can be done. With a parent at home you no longer have to pay for daycare, nannies, or baby-sitters. He/she can also do the budgeting, shopping, coupon clipping, home repairs, computer repair, yard work, etc., saving thousands of dollars, allowing the family to get by on even less. And other efficiencies will manifest themselves as you won't have to pay for therapists (because your children were brought up right), your wife is less likely to divorce you (saving on massive legal costs), and the stay at home parent can pursue entrepreneurial ventures in their free time (potentially earning even more money than the working parent).

The point is the onus and focus should not be on "making enough money" to afford children. It should be focused on "saving enough money" so that you can afford a stay-at-home parent.

#4 No Divorce

If you get married, don't have children, and then decide to get divorced, that's a sad, but victimless mistake.

If you get married, HAVE children, and then get divorced, that's child abuse. And there's no other way around it. You hurt your children when you get divorced and you should feel absolutely ashamed and disgusted with yourself. Not only for getting divorced, but for choosing so poorly a person to bring children into the world with.

Sadly, society celebrates divorce, particularly women. It's "empowering," "you go girl," and "girl power!" Which is all fine and good AS LONG AS THERE ARE NO CHILDREN INVOLVED. But once you have children, remember, your life is over. All that matters is the children's lives. And that goes for both your life and your wife's.

Because of this, if you "want to do the right thing" you will do at least the simplest of courtesies to your children and "fake it" until they turn 18 and move out of the house. I've known more than one couple who wanted to get divorced, but didn't because of their children. They stayed together, putting on the charade for nearly two decades (even having separate dating lives) all for the sake of their children. Then, when the last child graduated from high school, they announced their divorce.

Naturally, this isn't always an option as there are some spouses that are so horribly behaved they're a threat to the children. And in these cases divorce is called for. But if both parents are sane and can at least put on the facade of a stable nuclear family, it certainly is a hell of a lot better than dropping the divorce bomb on your five and three year old children, destroying their sense of security and ruining their childhoods forever.

#5 Tough, Fatherly Love

No matter what the media tells you,
No matter what politicians say
And no matter what Oprah says,

Families need fathers.

This "heroic single mother" bullshit is precisely that – bullshit.

Because of a myriad of reasons (beyond the scope of this book) there is a social, political, and economic push to marginalize fathers in today's society, belittling the role they play in both society and the family. In return, they exalt single motherhood, single parenthood, and pretty much any other form of the family as long as it isn't the normal, nuclear family, and as long as it doesn't have a father.

Unfortunately, this skewed approach has had the disastrous consequences you'd expect it to have when you more or less dismiss or kick out an entire sex from society. Divorce, broken families, broken children, crime, psychological problems, recession, lower economic growth, increased bankruptcies, drug addiction, alcoholism, you name it, nearly every problem we have today in the US is (*at least* in-part) due to the lack of strong, manly fathers in today's families.

Thankfully, however, just because society is trending this way, doesn't mean you have to. And like all other decisions in life, if you make the right ones, your personal life will benefit from it. So when it comes to raising your children you have to ignore what society says and KNOW that children NEED their fathers and they need tough fatherly love.

Of course, children can't just get by on "tough, fatherly love." They need both the nourishing, forgiving, kind, sweet love from their mother and the disciplinarian, patriarchical love from their father. But right now society is so skewed towards the motherly "bribe you with cake" method of rearing that children are being ill-reared. This not only gives you the right to mete out the tough, fatherly love, but a mandate.

What this tough, fatherly love is though, is simple. It's the love that is more concerned with your children 30 years from now, than you are about them today. So while the mother is tending to all the immediate needs of her children *today* (food, injuries, care, emotions, etc.), as a father it is your responsibility to train them, prepare them, and equip them to survive as adults into *tomorrow*.

Sadly, this is not the "cookies and cake" sort of love the mother gets to deal out, but it is no less important. It is telling your child no, disciplining and punishing them if they display aberrant behavior that will get them hurt and killed in the future, and ensuring they do not get too full of themselves so they might function well with other adults. But the real value of fatherly love is the wisdom, guidance, and context they will need to navigate and be successful in life.

For example, my insistence on humans being the most important thing in life, and your wife/children being the most important human beings, is the context necessary for every human to go forth and get the most out of life. That context, however, is just not provided by mothers.

Another example was a female friend of mine whose dad would not pay her way through college unless she majored in a STEM field. At the time she hated him for it. He was "not letting her be herself." But in the end this WISDOM paid off greatly. She is now a doctor, does not live at home, and does not worry about poverty or strife.

And a third, lifting weights. When I was a teenage boy I was told by my mother that girls don't like jocks or big strong guys. They liked sensitive caring men. Men who listened to their problems. And all the other typical female bullshit women say. Of course, pursuing that strategy was a SPECTACULAR failure and led to absolutely NO success with women. It wasn't until I listened to one of my fatherly male elders did he provide me the guidance that women do not want sensitive, caring men, but strong, aloof, and indifferent men, no matter what they say. In the end I hit the gym (among other things) and improved my success with women dramatically.

The point is that your sons and daughters need strong, disciplined, and strategic long-term love. Because while motherly love is kind, forgiving, and absolutely necessary, it does NOTHING to prepare your children for the harsh realities of life that they are going to face in the future. And if you don't deliver this necessary love to them, they WILL suffer a life of confusion, failure, ineptitude, and strife because they were always pampered, never trained, hardened, or disciplined.

In short, it is the mother's love that ensures the child doesn't run away.
It is the father's love that ensures your child wants to come back home to visit you as an adult.

#6 Independence

Wisdom, guidance, leadership, and context aside, the ultimate goal of tough, fatherly love is to teach your kid independence. For in the end, this is not only the greatest gift you can give your children, but a necessary and vital one.

The problem, however, is that it is often too tempting for parents to "cop out," telling their children pretty lies instead of holding them to the standards of harsh reality. Thus why you have parents who spoil their children rotten, never telling them no, being their "BFF," instead of being their god damned parents. Sadly, while this may make things "peaceful" and avoid confrontation with your children during childhood, you are misleading them about the real world. And when they finally reach it, they will have a huge disadvantage because they are incapable of supporting themselves and really do think the world owes them a living.

Sadly, there are many institutions and entities that are more than willing to take advantage of your children's naivety, perpetuating this lie. Politicians are more than happy to tell people they're entitled to things (as long as they get their vote). Banks and mortgage companies will lend money to people who can't afford it, as long as they get those late fees and can repossess the house. And the movie and media industries are only all too happy to tell your children "they can have it all" even if they can't make rent. The result is not a life of "leisure" where your child is adequately cared for with monies that he or she is entitled to, but one of the typical person who does not support themselves:

Bill collectors constantly hounding them.
The IRS threatening them with fines or jail.
Worrying about whether they'll make rent or get evicted.
Taking public transportation because they can't afford a car.
Worrying about how they're going to pay off their $80,000 in student loans.

This is the life you will condemn your child to unless you teach them the importance, value, and necessity of independence. No father, who truly loves his children, would ever wish that kind of life upon them. Ensure that doesn't happen. Ensure you raise independent children.

CHAPTER 10
LEGACY

The sad thing about life is that it ends. One day you're here, with your loving wife and kids, money in the bank, convertible in the garage, and then SPLAT!!!! You're hit by a bus. Again, nobody knows when they're going to go, so all you can do is your best and hope for good luck and health. But there's a bit of irony in being finite or mortal.

While you may end, the rest of the world won't. It will go on forever.

This presents, arguably, the most interesting predicament to every person alive. While the part of human history most important to you was when you were alive, the truth is the most important part your life will play in human history is in the future when you are dead. Specifically, what kind of legacy did you leave behind?

Regardless of your religious beliefs, whether you're up in heaven looking down or you completely and totally cease to exist in any realm or form, once your time is up here that is all you can do to influence the world. And while you may have ended, the world won't and your effects on the planet will last on into forever. This isn't to say that you didn't influence the world while you were alive, but that the vast majority of your influence will be after you're dead. Ergo, the importance of leaving a good legacy.

There are many aspects to a legacy as there are to life. Were you a good dog groomer? Did you like coffee? How good were you at GTAV? Did you prefer redheads? But ultimately the legacy you leave behind, your immortal reputation by which the future generations will remember and judge you by, boils down to three key things;

Your Family
Your Country/Community
Your Personal Works

And it is focusing on these three things that will determine the value, quality, and character of your "final act."

Your Family

A huge part of your legacy will be your family because not only are they likely to be the most important people in your life (and therefore know you better than anybody else), but because you also most likely brought some children into this world, heavily influencing them as well. These children will continue on after you pass away, conveying your legacy onto friends, family, and even their children.

The question is how do you want your family and future descendants remembering you?

Were you a strong, providing, and supporting father? The pillar of your family whose wisdom, love, guidance, and support produced equally productive and loving children? A husband or boyfriend who made his woman happy, providing her a life of laughter, fun, and an adventure she'll never forget?

Or were you a deadbeat dad? A guy who stuck his dick in a whole full of crazy? An absentee father who brought a dozen unwanted children into the world he couldn't afford and didn't care about? A drifter whose effective family consisted of him and him alone and will never be remembered, let alone WANT TO BE remembered by his children and the people in his life?

Again, nobody can force you to care about what happens after you die. But you can either be lovingly remembered for generations to come or just plain forgotten because nobody cared...or worse, an example your children, family, and society points to and says, "don't be like that fuck up."

Your Country/Community

Obviously, it is not just your family you will have an influence on. There are friends, co-workers, colleagues, and many other people your life will affect. However, because we live in a democracy you have an added responsibility to your country and community.

Specifically, you have the right to vote which means you are ultimately responsible for the direction and success of this nation.

This is important because (once again) after you pass away your family, friends, children, and any other loved ones will continue on, living in the country YOU voted in while you were alive. Thus, you, me, and everybody else owe it to our loved ones to inform ourselves about economics, politics, government, history, etc., so we can ensure they live in a country that is free, safe, and growing economically.

I have tried my best to avoid discussing politics in this book when unnecessary. However, to be blunt and for the sake of efficiency, the black community REALLY needs to wake up when it comes to this. Despite 50 years of "The Great Society" and socialist government help, black standards of living have simply not improved relative to white standards of living. You need to set aside pride, ego, and emotion, and ask yourself "is what we're doing working?" Not for any political reasons. Not to support the "Republicans" or "Democrats." But for the sake of you while you're on this planet and for the sake of loved ones after you leave. And while I cannot present a thorough and complete economic argument in this one chapter (let alone an entirely separate book), all I ask is that you take a SCIENTIFIC look at the political policies that have been enacted in Detroit, East St. Louis, South Side Chicago, Compton, and other predominantly black communities/cities, and see if that has been working.

In the end, hopefully, you will educate yourself to see what is truly going on, which will allow for a MUCH BETTER future for you and your loved ones.

Your Personal Works

Family is certainly great. Being an informed, educated patriot, loyal to your country and community is also great. But none of this speaks to you and your own individual accomplishments. And while this is not an argument to be selfish, ignoring your family, only focusing on the things you like, you deserve to have at least part of your legacy be about your specific accomplishments and interests.

What this is varies greatly and is completely up to you. Henry Ford's legacy was the automobile. My grandpa's legacy was being a mortician. Michael Jordan's legacy will be being a better basketball player than LeBron James ever was. And my legacy will likely be my books. Whatever it is, with our intellects, brains, and individualities, every man should leave something to this world special and unique to him.

The key thing, however, is to realize it doesn't have to be famous or glorious. Entertaining as Jordan and LeBron are, in the end, they just dunk an orange sphere into a red ring "real good." They're not curing cancer. They're not creating electricity. But they don't have to be and neither do you.

Wood carving.
Creating music.
Lifting weights.
Marksmanship.
Cooking.
Charcuterie.
Fishing.

Something that you personally enjoy and excel at. Something you do so well it improves and inspires other people's lives. So well when you pass on people will say,

"You know, not only was a he a great father, husband, and friend, but he left behind some damn fine paintings."

It doesn't have to be great, it just has to be you.

Your Legacy

Add all those things up and that is your legacy. Your reputation. What will last long after you are gone. Do you want future young black men looking up to you, citing you as a hero they wish and aspire to be like? Do you want ALL young men to look up to you, saying, "there is a man that I want to become?" Perhaps you are the future leader of the black community who leads his fellow black men to outperform Asians as the top engineers and earners in the country. Perhaps you are the guy that will cure cancer. But none of that will come true if you accept your current lot in life. None of that will ever be achieved if you accept mediocrity, victimhood, commonness, and self-pity. You get one shot at life an as the great William Shatner said,

"You are going to die."

Do not squander it.

Resources:

www.avoiceformen.com
www.blowmeuptom.com
www.victoryunlimitedshow.com
www.returnofkings.com
www.freedomainradio.com
heartiste.wordpress.com
www.newsninja2012.com
www.youtube.com/user/MrGlendoncameron
www.hermancain.com
www.allenbwest.com
www.rooshv.com
www.socraddockmethod.com
www.daveramsey.com

You may also be interested in the following
finance/investment/retirement planning classes offered by the author:

www.ed2go.com/online-courses/stocks-bonds-and-investing-oh-my
www.ed2go.com/online-courses/analysis-and-valuation-of-stocks

Special Thanks To:

Vincent Kelly
Marlon Dixon
Marcus Brown
Glendon Cameron
Jay Nix
Curtis Williams

Whose advice and experience helped guide and forge this book.

Books/Media You May Also Like:

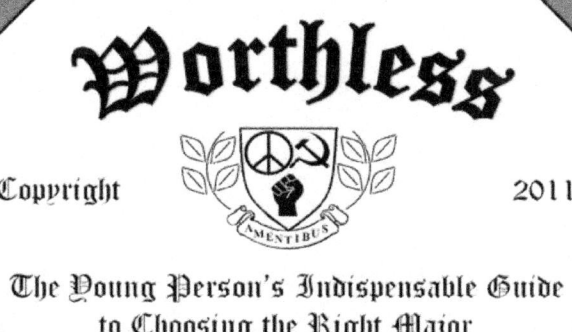

DON'T CHOOSE A STUPID MAJOR!

Buy "Worthless"

Available on Amazon!

www.assholeconsulting.com

WELCOME TO
THE DIVIDE...
.S.P. DALEY

CONFESSIONS
OF AN
ONLINE HUSTLER

How to Make Money and Become
an Internet Superstar

Matt Forney

Printed in Great Britain
by Amazon